I0617966

CHRIST CAME
to
DESTROY
THE WORK OF
SATAN

APOSTLE DE BURNEY

CHRIST CAME TO DESTROY THE WORKS OF SATAN

THUS,

"BY REMOVING THE PENALTY OF SIN, SO WE CAN
BE IN RIGHT STANDING WITH GOD?"

Copyright © 2023 Apostle De Burney

Apostle3477@gmail.com

ISBN: 978-1-960704-01-6

All rights reserved. No part of this publication may be reproduced or transmitted in any form or by any means, mechanical or electronic, including photocopying or recording, or by any information storage and retrieval system, or transmitted by email without permission in writing from the publisher.

While all attempts have been made to verify the information provided in this publication, neither the author nor the publisher assumes any responsibility for errors, omissions, or contrary interpretations of the subject matter herein.

This book is for education purposes only. The views expressed are those of the author alone and should not be taken as expert in-struction or commands. The reader is responsible for his or her own actions.

Adherence to all applicable laws and regulations, including in-ternational, federal, state, and local governing professional licensing, business practices, advertising, and all other aspects of doing business in the US, Canada, or any other jurisdiction is the sole responsibility of the purchaser or reader

Table of Contents

CHAPTER 1

JESUS CAME TO DESTROY THE WORK OF SATAN

I John 3:8 NKJV

8 He who Sins is of the devil, for the devil has Sinned from the beginning. For this purpose, the Son of God was manifested, that He might destroy the works of the devil.

As we can see from the scripture, the devil is the one that brought sin to the world. The first man that Sinned as we know is Adam through his wife who was deceived by the devil by making her eat the forbidden fruit (Genesis3:1-9). But we have been saved by his Son Jesus Christ who was crucified on the cross to make atonement for our Sins. Ascending to heaven, Michael, cast the devil from heaven and to earth. Jesus came to destroy the works of the devil. And that work is the fear of death and Sins that enslaves us all. By conquering death, Jesus freed us from the bondage of fear of death and delivered us from Sin. Now we no longer live by the fear that leads to Sin. We seek to live out of love, which, when perfected, dispels all fear (1 John 4: 8).

Jesus came to destroy the works of the devil according to God's plan. God created "eternal fire" for "the devil and his angels." So following the devil means then destroying him forever. Hence, Jesus broke the devil's schemes at the cross. Our three enemies are Satan, Sin, and Death. Satan uses the latter two (sin and death) as powers to enslave and destroy us {Rom 6}. When we agree with Satan, we show that he is our father {John 8:44}. He was a liar from the beginning and leads the world and its powers to deceive and perish the world forever. John writes, "We know that we are of God, and the whole world lies in wickedness" {1 John 5:19}. Jesus brings us from the kingdom of darkness to the kingdom of light {Col 1:13}. We enter the kingdom of God, which is the presence of God and his Son Christ - light from light. Until the end, we live on the highway in a struggle for virtue. To love God, and do good anguishes the enemy who wants to deceive us, force us to lie, ruin what is good, and turn it into a flawed servant of God. Because he was cast out of heaven, Satan rages against the church like a roaring lion. But we have the crown of victory over him in Christ, that we may overcome sin: "We know that whosoever is born of God sinned not: but he that is begotten of God kept himself, and that wicked one touched him not" {1 John 5:18}. Only the gospel can restore us or give birth to God so that we can defeat the devil and his works through Christ. This is the message that the New Testament emphasizes.

CHAPTER 2

WHAT IS THE WORK OF SATAN?
SIN!!

Which disconnected us from God?

What are the "works" of Satan? *Morally* he tempts us to sin. If you are a Christian. *Physically*, he causes disease and seeks to destroy those who have the image of God. *Intellectually*, he seduces us with mistakes. And *spiritually* he blinds the minds of unbelievers so that they do not see and believe the gospel. Satan and his army fought against humanity, but it was sad that many Christians did not realize the scale of this war. This spiritual and biblical war teaches a lot about the work of enemies and spiritual warfare. The devil tempts us to sin. If you are a Christian, he physically causes disease and seeks to destroy those who bear the image of God. Intellectually, he seduces us with mistakes. In addition, he deeply blinds the psyche of unbelievers if they see and accept the gospel. On the planet, Satan uses money, sex, and opportunities to protect many people from knowing God through his

Son, Jesus Christ. Money is the backbone of all needs; so many malicious and indescribable difficulties for products are caused by money. Satan and his powers work in all four corners so that people are far from knowing God. Perhaps praying for a question without an answer for a while, then the adversary will reveal to you that your God cannot answer your prayers, and on the other hand, at that time you will be against the enemy. Your trust in God will decline. Satan loves what God despises; for example, God says, "I despise separation," and Satan will say, "I love alone." Satan can keep you from misery. Satan can remove your well-being, which can add to suffering and discouragement. Satan is awkward and clever, so we can simply attack him with a name that is above another name in paradise, on earth, or under the earth, which is Jesus Christ.

CHAPTER 3

WHAT PUTS US INTO SIN?

The Law

1 Corinthians 15: 56 amp.

The Bible Says the Strength of Sin Is the Law "The sting of DEATH is SIN, and the strength of SIN IS THE LAW."

56 For sin is the sting that results in death, and the law gives sin its power.

57 But thank God! He gives us victory over sin and death through our Lord Jesus Christ.

What the scripture is saying above is that sin does not have dominion over us because Jesus has eradicated the law through his blood by making us a living soul by his death he paid on the cross. The apostle Paul personifies death as a living being and using sin to cause death, either as a string or a hint by which he causes mortal suffering. The notion is that the cause of death is sin. It introduced him; it makes it real; it is the cause of the pain, suffering, and horror that befalls him. If there were no sin, people would not have died. Without sin, death would not be met with horror or anxiety. Why should the innocent be afraid to die? Why the innocent needs to be feared anywhere in the universe of the righteous God? Therefore, the fact that people die is proof that they are sinners; the fact that they feel horror and anxiety is proof that they feel guilty and that they are afraid to come into the presence of a holy God. If it is taken away, if sin is removed, it will certainly remove both the horror and the pity and the danger it can cause.

How did sin become so powerful? Paul is clear: the power of sin — that is, the ability to cause death — comes from the law. By law, Paul means both the law of Moses given to Israel and the nature of mankind to rebel against God, which was first revealed when Adam and Eve Sinned against the command of God in the Garden (Genesis 3: 17-19). It is not the case that the law creates sin for men. The law reveals sin by showing that people are incapable of obeying God. According to any commandment of God, it is our nature to rebel, to sin. In this way, it is shown that all are sinful (Romans 3:23), and all are deserving of death (Romans 6:23). Praise God, which is not the end of history, as this verse reveals (1 Corinthians 15: 50–58 powerfully concludes Paul's teaching on the resurrection of Christians: when the last trumpet is heard and Christ returns for those who belong to Him. At that moment, all believers in Jesus, living and dead will be transformed into the glorified, eternal bodies promised to us. Death will be defeated forever, never to harm anyone again. Sin brings death, and the force of sin is the law, but by forgiving our sin by faith in Jesus and His grace, God has given us victory over death.

Paul emphasizes that the newness of life in Christ liberates us from being "captive" to the "old composed code" of the law (Rom. 7:6). All things being considered, Paul concludes, the issue is God's contradicting power he calls "sin" moving to people. Sin's capacity isn't only settling on terrible decisions nor doing things do we realize we shouldn't. For instance, an abhorrent force has attacked the domain of every individual's soul and takes control, "sold into bondage under wrongdoing," as Paul puts it under this servitude to sin, and we can't do the great called for in the rules and known in our souls. This happens notwithstanding, our honest goal is to do what God wants. As such, information on what is acceptable isn't sufficient to defeat the intensity of transgression that has attacked us! For I do not do the unique thing which I need, but the contemptible thing that I need not, which is my primary concern" (Rom 7:19). We can guard against this predicament simply by intercepting another, even more wonderful, power, the Holy Spirit, which is turning into a concentration for the Romans 8. We know very well that understanding what God needs is not enough to sustain us in a work environment. . For example, in any case, when we know well in our minds that God needs us to treat everyone differently, we sometimes experience a sacrifice of fictitious insight that we could prophesy by speaking ineffectively about an accomplice. In addition, mothers and fathers, when creating upbringing, understand that shouting outrage at a young child is not acceptable. But now sometimes the intensity of the violations overwhelms them, and they do it anyway. A legal adviser who charges clients for administration is constantly aware that he should handle time accounting carefully, but in any case, may be overwhelmed by irregularities in order to mitigate his working hours in order to increase his salary.

We alone are particularly powerless against the intensity of illegal action within us. In any of our workplaces, it would be good if we looked for others and helped each other resist this force that is trying to defeat our will to make the smartest and greatest decision. For example, there is still a slight increase in the number of Christians who join the small friends of people working in similar circumstances. Extra bunches meet anywhere from an hour once a week, grinding places regularly, to a big day to day once a month. People focus on revealing to each other the subtleties of the circumstances they face at work and talking about them in terms of trust, making choices, and being determined to pursue action plans. The part may depict a dispute with an accomplice, a moral slip, a sense of meaninglessness, an organizational strategy that seems unfounded. After drawing on other knowledge, some would focus on the game plan and report back to the meetings on the outcome of future gatherings.

CHAPTER 4

HOW DID CHRIST TAKE AWAY OUR SIN?

By Dying On The Cross and Removing the Law

1 John 1:7, NIV:

(Blood of Jesus takes us from all sin)

7 *"But if we walk in the light, as he is in the light, we have fellowship with one another, and the BLOOD OF JESUS, his Son, PURIFIES us from ALL SIN."*

Christ came into this world to die for us on the cross, thus reconciling our sins, which again rendered the law ineffective. When the Holy Spirit shone forth on the children of God, we have a true vision and intuition of sin. First, when the Holy Spirit has been condemned for sin, righteousness, and judgment, we are faced with our flaws and utter sinfulness. When we are enlightened by the truths of the gospel, we begin to realize the great price Christ paid for us on the cross — because only faith in the blood of Jesus

Christ, the only Son of God, forgives us our sins and sin — only through his shed blood do we cleanse ourselves from all sin. Only by grace through faith are we called out of the darkness of sin and death into the wonderful light of His righteousness and life. Only by believing in the finished work of Christ Calvary can we enter the room of the throne of grace and if we abide in Him and walk in the light of His love, we will associate with our heavenly Father because of the blood of his Son Jesus who saved us and who continues to cleanse us from all sin.

When we walk with God in the light of his love, we rejoice in mutual fellowship with the Father. The more time we remain in His Company, the more we are like Him. He does not conform to our image, but we are transformed into his image and beauty. And the more we walk in the light of His own light, the more truth and righteousness, the more we will become like Jesus. Once upon a time we were filled with darkness and we walked the path of the world, but we are not out of the world. John asks, "What communion does light have with darkness? What communion can a holy God have with a fallen sinner?" During salvation, we were enlightened by the truth of the glorious gospel of grace and by faith; we became bright in the Lord and are called to walk as children of light.

To walk in the light means to live according to His perfect life and character. We must avoid evil and sustain ourselves in righteousness and truth by obedience to His guidance and direction. Darkness can never obscure God's light because the darkness is simply the absence of God's light the absence of God. After all, there is no darkness in it at all. When we remain in His realm of light and truth, the former darkness that has enslaved us can never challenge us, because if we go in the Light, we are not in the realm of darkness. For salvation, we can immediately enter into the presence of God, and by walking in the light we are allowed to enjoy a lovely communion with the

Heavenly Father. Unfortunately, when we choose not to walk in the light, we lose that privilege. Saved but from communion with the Father.

When we were brought to the light of God at the time of salvation, the cross was treated not only with the remission of our former sins. We have received the ultimate purification of every transgression — past, present, and future — the removal of all our known and unknown sins into the sea of God's gracious forgetfulness — over time and into eternity. Because of his complete identification with our sin, we are fully identified with the light of the Lord and the righteousness of Christ. He makes us perfect and holy in His sight. It is positional holiness that ends from the very first moment we believed. It is a cleansing flood that has become our faith in Jesus. It is attributed righteousness that we do not deserve, but which is our gift as the free and wonderful grace of God. All of this is accomplished in only one way by faith freely sacrificing the blood of the perfect human sacrifice, our Savior Jesus Christ. This can only be obtained by believing in the sacrifice of a pure, holy, harmless, innocent sacrifice ... whose shed blood cleanses the cursed sinner, redeems the wicked, and forgives the guilty, while delivering God's hated condemned sinner eternal condemnation.

Only the divine sacrifice for the holy Son of God, who by incarnation freely assumed the mortal body to identify with his condemned brethren, is a sufficient reward for the accumulated sin of the whole world. Only the blood of Christ can abolish the power of sin and Satan, pain and disease, destruction, death, and hell itself. Only the mighty blood of the Holy Lamb of God can break the chains of sin and release the captive. Only by believing in the work done by Christ can God declare a sinner to be saved? There is power in the blood of Jesus in the precious blood of the Lamb of God; there is a POWER that works miracles. Given our great salvation, of course, it should be our heart's deepest desire to walk in the light, as HE is in the light, to maintain communion with our Father, for the blood of Jesus, His Son, continues to purify us day after day.

First, believers will have community and friendship. Second, believers will experience forgiveness. Although man is (eternally) forgiven of his sins when he first believes in Christ, Christians still commit sins and need forgiveness as believers. Even the apostle Paul noted his many failures, despite his desire to live righteously, and the many noble deeds he did for God (Romans 7).

The effect here is clear: the mere presence of sin in a person's life does not mean that a person is lost. Christ's sacrifice abolishes the eternal punishment of all sins, past, present, and future. More importantly, those who trust in Christ is forgiven even for the sins they do not know. We should confess the sins we learn of and be forgiven. That recipe, presented differently, is the main point of what we talk about Jesus. What does this mean? How does his blood he shared cleanse our own sin? How can one person remove sin from the world? When trying to respond to this, we should be careful not to fall into the typical misconception. Certain methods of Scripture and doctrines for reporting this may give the impression that the suffering and transmission of Jesus eliminated the transgressions of the world in one way or other by caring for a commitment to God, specifically that God took Jesus. "Poor as a reward for our wrongdoing — it shows that God lived from Adam's transgression in frustration, sitting down so that someone could pay enough of the obligation before that transgression could be forgiven. The photographs and analogies used to communicate Jesus 'transgression can make such an impression whenever it is made in the true sense, but that's not what they mean.

This idea is deeply grounded: many pre-Christian societies had customs, including surrogacy. It was not sanctioned in a similar way in every place, but it was basically similar to the following: At regular intervals, the network will try to clear itself of the customs of obscenity (fragmentation, disputes, jealousy, malice, fights, burglary, resentment, murder, etc.), designed to remove these things from the world. The custom goes this way: they would take a goat and metaphorically load on their back, through a certain image (which often involved hanging a goat in purple and putting a crown of thorns on its head) what they thought was wrong in their locality.

The goat was then exiled to the desert to pass it on. The idea was that the goat would take away the damage to the net. Poorly, it usually had specific viability. There was greater solidarity for those gathered for a period of time. No real change has taken place. Nothing has really changed. Jealousy and resentment remained as before, regardless of whether people had the opportunity to live correspondingly friendlier for a period of time. How at that time did Jesus, the slain sheep, remove sin from the world? Jesus, as the sheep of God, does not eradicate the transgressions of the world by taking it away in one way or another, so it does not exist in the world right now. He removes it by changing, perfecting, accepting into himself, and changing. We see cases of all this throughout his life, though this is usually shown by the love and absolute he shows in his passing hour. Clearly, Jesus removed the transgression from the world by accepting contempt and offering love back; depriving resentment and contemplation; accepting jealousy and giving a gift; accepting austerity and providing warmth; accepting insignificance and offering backward empathy; he accepts chaos and offers back harmony; and by taking illegal actions and offering retroactivity. This is definitely not something easy to do. What easily falls into place is the offer to return in kind: contempt for contempt, indignation with indignation, vivacity for frigidity, and reward for hurt. Someone is hitting us, so we hit back. But at that time, sin remains in the world, and no action of redemption, ritualized informality, or anything else is a real stimulus for changing things, because we don't change anything, moreover, we go as channels transmitting the indistinguishable energy that continues to us.

Jesus did something else. He gave not only what was done to him. Or maybe it took, kept, passed on, changed, and eventually returned as something else. It is the thing that establishes his peaceful attachment, or more precisely, the torturous suffering (from the cross) that he had to endure in order to resent and offer worship. However, this is the only way a violation can leave the world. Someone has to accept it, hold it, pass it on, and replace it with another through some unbearable self-repentance. So Christianity, among all the world's religions and methods of reasoning, is the religion that loves substitution. Moreover, this dynamic is not just what we are turning to in Jesus. Manifestation is meant to progress. We appeal to continue to offer material to God and to continue to do what Jesus did. Later, our task is also.

CHAPTER 5

WHEN CHRIST REMOVED THE LAW, HE DESTROYED THE WORKS OF SATAN BY REMOVING THE CONSEQUENCES OF SIN

Romans 4:14–15 AMP

14 If those who are followers of the Law are the true heirs of Abraham, then faith leading to salvation] is of no effect and void, and the promise of God is nullified.

15 For the Law results in God's wrath against sin, but where there is no law, there is no violation or consequences of it either].

Romans 10:4 (NKJV)

10 For Christ is the END OF THE LAW for RIGHTEOUSNESS to everyone who BELIEVES.

In the words of the scripture above, we can see quite possibly the main undertakings of Jesus have been uncovered to us. Verses 14–15 show that if salvation comes according to the law, it destroys both faith and promise. Faith in work-oriented salvation is not necessary. It would also remove the principle of God's promise, the sacrifice of grace. The Romans are the ones who keep the "law." These are people who live by the law as the way of salvation. These individuals are more than Jews; they are all trying to keep the laws of salvation. There is no salvation in the law. Paul established the law and the promise. If you break one, you have broken them all. God's standards show people that they can never live up to the expectations of the law. That failure should lead them to seek the principle of faith.

If Jews have acquired the right to the eyes of God by law, it has a serious impact on how people become Christians. Salvation would happen not just by faith, but by something else. That would make a void of the faith, as we see in another phrase. Faith void remains vanity, The Holy Spirit used two strict terms to deny the salvation of creation: "made nothing" and "made of no effect." There are then two justifications for justifying a law. The first is that it permanently invalidates faith. If we become Christians by the law, we will not have to come to God by "faith." The Greek word "invalidated" is empty, rendered meaningless, and becomes invalid. Faith would be emptied. The time of the Greek language indicates that the result would be that the faith would remain in a permanent state of disability (by the law). Faith by the law in that case would have no value in salvation. The word "faith" has a definite article, which goes back to Abraham's faith. His faith would remain permanently invalid based on the hypothesis of justification by the law (perfect time). Any idea that people are justified by works loses faith as a proper principle of salvation. Faith has no value if we accept God's promises according to the law. All of this empty's faith in its essential sense. If God saves people by the law, by keeping the law, then there is no place for Faith in Christ.

The second consequence of being saved by the law is that the promise becomes ineffective. The word "promise" occurs four times in verses 13-22. The promise does not depend on compliance with the law. This would refute the idea of an unconditional promise. From the point of view of the law, the "promise" of God does not work. Any other promise invalidates the promise of God; the promise must be unconditional, otherwise, it would not be a promise. If we ask for anything more than faith in God's promise, we will cancel the promise.

A promise is an unconditional commitment to someone. Faith is trust in that promise. Abraham's faith was an appropriate response to God's promise. Promises are two Greek words: (1) the first conveys the idea of a promise, which includes certain conditions; (2) the second is an unconditional promise made out of the principle of grace to men. The second is a Greek word in this verse. God loves us unconditionally. His love will sometimes make us happy and sometimes sad, but it still loves. It is a love that will never let us go. It is love that does not depend on us or our merits, but entirely on God's heart for us. Paul discusses God's promises to Abraham and his offspring, the Jewish people. This is what God gave in Genesis 12: 1–3. These promises, written by Paul, amount to Israel being the heirs of the world. Now Paul is showing that this inheritance will not be carried out under the law. In particular, these promises were made centuries before the law came into force. Paul writes that if an inheritance is to be given to those who keep the law, then faith is irrelevant. Worse, God's promises don't matter - because not all of Abraham's descendants had the law!

In other words, Paul has already shown that no one can keep the law. All sinned and did not attain the glory of God (Romans 3:10; 3:23). So, if God's promises to Israel are only for those who can keep the law, those promises will not be given. When the law is a requirement of salvation, faith has no purpose He came from paradise to earth to decimate crafted by the demon. The happenings to Jesus were, it could be said, a mission. The evil domain of dimness had set up itself here on earth, assembled its strongholds and defenses, cast a weighty spell on individuals, oppressed and tortured them. The fortresses behind which Satan stows away are more grounded than the dividers of Jericho, which are twenty meters high and twelve meters wide. Human strength isn't sufficient to put them down.

There must be somebody more grounded than we are. Also, he showed up: Jesus, the Son of God. He saw crafted by the fallen angel in the hearts and networks of people groups like no other. Jesus took up the battle against Satan. We can be certain that he will likewise totally satisfy his errand, for Almighty God showed up in him. This is a bit of our Christmas euphoria. Right up till today the world is still brimming with being crafted by Satan. This is especially apparent in crafted by Satan since he is the father of falsehoods. How individuals lie nowadays! The truth is spreading in legislative issues, in exchange, in business life. Individuals lie out of personal circumstance, out of dread, out of politeness. The fiend is a haughty soul. Consequently, all the vanity, the pride, the stomping on of the feeble to transcend their wretchedness. Satan is likewise the informer of the siblings. Consequently, all the contentions and quarrels, the contempt and the harshness. You nearly need to surrender at seeing all the fiend's chips away at the earth. Yet, the word remains: Jesus is the victor! This word will be satisfied in the battle against Satan as unquestionably as light is more grounded than dimness.

God's Son became man to destroy the works crafted by the devil (1 John 3: 8) and to convey us from wrongdoing, death, and the devil. This he achieved when he died on the cross. From that point onward, all who have confidence in his name have been named the sons of God and from the realm of the dimness of this world into the light of the realm of God. Jesus made us free and residents of paradise. With the end goal for individuals to understand what Jesus accomplished for them, he provided us the order to announce this happy message: "As the Father has sent me, so I send you." (John 20:21) he says: "See, I have given you the capacity to step on snakes and scorpions, and control over all excitement of the adversary, and nothing will hurt you" (Luke 10:19). Jesus gave to us what he got from the Father: the ability to decimate the demons works, for example, ailment, destitution, and languishing. At the point when we vow for Jesus and his work of recovery, crafted by Christ, he should likewise be uncovered through us. He went about blessed with Holy Spirit and force, doing great and mending all who were in the intensity of the demon, for God was with him. (Acts 10:38) - As the Father was with Jesus, so Jesus is with us now! The Lord favor you bounteously and lead you into the administration that wrecks the demon's works.

CHAPTER 6

WHERE THERE IS NO LAW, THERE IS NO SIN

Romans 5:13 (AMP)

(But Sin Is Not Charged Against Anyone When There Is No Law)

13 Sin was committed in the world before the Law was given, but sin is not charged against anyone when there is no law against it.

2 Corinthians 5:17- 19 NIV

(Because of Christ God is not counting your sins against you)

17 Therefore, if anyone is in Christ, the new creation has come: The old has gone, the new is here!

18 All this is from God, who reconciled us to himself through Christ and gave us the ministry of reconciliation:

19 that God was reconciling the world to himself in Christ, not counting people's sins against them. And he has committed to us the message of reconciliation.

What the verses in the chapter are saying is that when there is no law enforced on a believer, his/her sin cannot be counted against him. Sin has come to the world before the law was given. Paul compares the effects of sin from Adam to the effects of grace, Christ. In the previous verse, he noted that it was the actions of one person that brought death and sin into the lives of all mankind. It seems that Paul immediately removes the main point of this chapter. He raised it again in line 15. Here, however, he answers a question that may have arisen for some of his readers. How could sin have been before the Law of Moses? Paul seemed to say in Romans 4:15 that without the law there is no sin or "transgression." In the context, Paul did not state that there is no true sin, but only that the law cannot be literally "broken" unless it is applied correctly to it.

Here Paul again clarifies the point: not that sin did not exist before the Law of Moses. Of course, from the garden people have always sinned. Instead, Paul says that before the law, specific sins were not credited to specific people. It was not an offense in the sense to break the written words of the law; it is simply sinful humanity that has expressed its sinful nature: self-serving, damaging, deceptive, and immoral. The argument here, as in Romans 4:15, is entirely promising. Mankind does not acknowledge sin when God does not give us something like the law: in our minds, those sins are not "counted." They are still sins because we should still know better (Romans 1: 18–20). The presence of the law does not turn justice into sin - it turns alleged ignorance into certain knowledge of our own wrongdoing.

Paul showed that the sinful nature in which every human being was born resulted in separation from God and inevitable death. Paul was disclosing to his readers that the explanation passing rules over all individuals are because all individuals have trespassed. At the end of the day, the result of violating God's law is demise. Be that as it may, according to Paul, there is a small question. Everyone understands that Adam broke God's command not to eat from the tree of the knowledge of good and evil, so it becomes clear why Adam kicked the bucket. Everyone also understands that after God gave His law to Moses on Mount Sinai, all the inhabitants of the earth somehow transgressed God's law (Rom. 3: 9-23).

Anyway, shouldn't something be said about the time between Adam and Moses? God had not directed those persons. There was no law of God created or spoken that they could break. So they could not transgress any law of God because they had no law. But then they still died. Why? Paul tries to explain why in Romans 5:13 and the passages that cover them. His main statement in all his assertions is that although the persons from Adam to Moses did not sin by breaking the order (as Adam did), they suffered the results of the transgression (transition). Why? From all the transgressions of Adam, sin (and later death) passed from Adam to all persons (Rom. 5:12

One sin of Adam bore sin and passed on to all mankind, which was not currently fertilized. He made his mind unconscious, realizing neither the results nor the individual, God will against whom he rebelled. Jesus knew from the beginning about the transgressions of all mankind and all the great havoc that would happen because of sin. He chose even before he made the world a symbol of redemption that would eradicate that injustice and revive the world. The consequences of Adam's transgression were far-reaching, even in the lives of people who never knew about him. They were confused, the consequence of Christ's gift is only general, because everyone who receives it as Savior will be saved. However, not every person gets it when they hear the uplifted new and not even every person will hear it.

Jesus said in John 5:24 that he who hears and trusts in him has eternal life. They are given eternal life quickly and permanently. The Holy Spirit dwells in them, and He, the Holy Spirit, immediately begins to tidy the room and project. In Genesis 4: 7 we can see where that equivalent offer was made to Cain, but he rejected it. God said, "Sin lies in the accesses, and its longing for you (to rule you), but you will rule it." You have to reign all your daily life. We will discuss this again in the not too distant future, as it is further mentioned in Revelation 5:10, as in the different chapters. Here we see that persons who sin without the law are the same as those who have broken the law. Sin will be, whether it is known to the guilty party or not. Individual information or the lack of that section does not affect the idea of illegal activity. In any case, individual sin is not included in the record of the offender unless the laws of God are known.

A person who violates God's law is intentionally responsible for conspiracy demonstrations to the creators. He has no basis for his disobedience. However, how does a person living apart from the rules about the law become guilty of transgression? In fact, no man on earth really has any reason for their illegal actions. This is because the ethical law consists of every heart. Man is created in the image and likeness of God from an ethical perspective. All persons, wherever there is natural light, control them.

A quiet, small voice testifies to a man's perceived considerations or deeds that are acceptable or bad. God did not leave man in complete obscurity. The soul will either forgive his behavior for doing well in the face of great thought processes, or will probably accuse him of doing evil with contemptuous purposes and, in any case, behaving well with low expectations. It will happen when he watches the eye of the extraordinary judge Jesus Christ on that incredible and terrible day when he decides for the hearts of the people. The heart will become a threatening observer to the insidious court decision, as this will confirm that their work is undervalued. A man's heart will condemn him to the wrath of God because of all his vigor.

CHAPTER 7

WHY GOD WON'T COUNT OUR SINS AGAINST US?

Because We Are Sanctified by the Blood of Jesus

1 John 1:7, NIV

Blood of Jesus takes us from all sin

7 *"But if we walk in the light, as he is in the light, we have fellowship with one another, and the BLOOD OF JESUS, his Son, PURIFIES us from ALL SIN."*

Basically, what that means is this. We sin but it's not counted against us now because Jesus paid the price with his blood. You are blessed today since every one of your sins is pardoned in Christ. God doesn't count your transgressions as a detriment to you. All things been equal, He makes you have a living life in Christ. That is the reason you are the honored man to whom the Lord doesn't and won't ascribe sin! What befalls such a man? We should take a gander at the tale of Jacob to discover.

The Bible records how Jacob deceived his father and deceived his elder brother and sister into giving his firstborn to Esau. (Genesis 27: 1–41.) Nevertheless, in spite of the wrong deceptive conduct, God chose to turn to Jacob. Besides, no, God didn't say to this word of deception, "You're a terrible criminal! How are you going to deceive your father? You're despised!" No, God did not please Jacob, "I am the God of your father Abraham, of the Lord, and of Isaac, the land on which you will lie, I will give it to you and to your loved ones. the earth, for I will not forsake you, till I have done that which I have said unto you." (Genesis 28: 13-15).

There was a man here to whom God did not attribute sin! God did not persuade Jacob in any way. All was taken into account, we heard Him say to Jacob, "I will take care of you, I am with you, I will keep you ... I will return, I will not leave you." Jacob did not positively deserve these gifts. If Jacob was so honored, it is the blood we share today with you and me who are under the new promise of beauty set by the blood of Jesus. The Blood is our blessing because Jesus removed all our sins at the cross! God does not attribute sin to you based on the work of Jesus. He attributes to you straightforwardness separate from his works. (Romans 4: 6.) And because you are noble, prepare for His grace! This instruction on grace can raise inquiries about God's judgment.

The truly sacred text states that God will judge the world and give it to every human being. How is this fact promising given what we have been discussing today? If you've seen a lot of dishonesty, I think you understand the requirement for a court order. The judgment is not really about dismissal or non-dismissal. It is associated with repairable items. It is associated with bringing truth and light to every territory. Men who do not respond to God's grace still remain in death. The fierceness of God contradicts the indecency itself. (Romans 1:18.) God's decision gives people a choice. (See, for example, Romans 1). Isaiah 61: 1-2 (NIV) The Spirit of the Lord GOD is upon me: for the LORD hath blessed me to preach the word unto the poor. He sent Christ to bind down and outward, to spread the opportunity for hostages and to release prisoners from the unknown, to proclaim the time of the Lord's goodness and the day of our God's reward. Note that this sacred text says the "year" of God's courtesy, but only His "day." Jesus stood in the temple and quoted this scripture but avoided saying "Our God's day of atonement." Then he said, "Today this holy text is satisfied with your hearing." (See Luke 4: 14–21.) Why didn't Jesus give it all? Because it was not the day of God's judgment. We tend to become like a beloved God. If we love God, who is a caring Father, we will cherish ourselves and reflect His love for other people. If we regard Him as a furious dictator, we will live in self-esteem and follow others according to the guidelines we try to live by. Although God is righteous and heavenly, and sin cannot match His quality, the question of our wrongdoing has been unequivocally addressed by the death of Jesus Christ. In the light of the cross, when God looks at us, he does not see our injustice, but only the precious blood of his Son. In light of Jesus 'repentance, we were adapted to God, and our transgressions were isolated from us as far as the east is from the west (Psalm 103: 12). What a great idea! God does not check my transgressions! God does not count your transgressions!

CHAPTER 8

IF YOU ARE BORN OF GOD YOU CANNOT SIN

I John 3:9 NKJV

(If You Are Born of God you cannot sin)

9 Whoever has been born of God does not sin, for His seed remains in him; and he cannot sin, because he has been born of God.

If we say that we are without mistakes, we distance ourselves and the fact of this problem is not in us. Even though we confess our transgressions, he is trustworthy and just, forgiving us for our wrongdoing and removing us from all iniquity.

If we say that we have not sinned, we describe him as a liar and his assertion is not in us. (1 John 1: 8–10; NIV). So we need to understand what John means in his remark in 1 John 3: 9. The point of John 1 John 3: 9 is basically that the changed offspring of God will have no behavior in trying to commit sin, and their way of life will satisfy the Lord Jesus and walk in common. way. of the Christian life. In any case, this does not mean impeccability.

This stage was preferred by the NIV over certain interpretations. For example, he understands KJV in the following directions: Who God did not renounce sin; for the seed remained in him, and he could not sin because it was designed by God. It's a bit of a contrast: "No one who is a descendant of God is constantly responsible for wrongdoing. He remains the undisputed pearl of life, and he cannot sin all the time - because he is a descendant of God. Nevertheless, at the moment, it is a real effort to be "free"; maybe it's too free. The most important thing to understand is that John is not writing anything here that he denies when everything is said and done 1 John 1: 8–10. Like Paul in Romans 7, John understands that none of us is great - far from him! - In any case, in Christ our lives really change. So "I can't sin" is a psychological / philosophical / deep remark, not relevant. It is also an additional thing that the change of God's descendants cannot be "sinners," because man is now in elegance and attributed to the sin committed. This means that a true Christian who finds something "bad" is not and never can be in a similar class to that man on the planet who rejects all of God's thoughts and "wrongdoings," that a person's transgressions are beyond doubt it is registered and the person will one day be in charge.

Some confuse these abstentions by saying that Christians can perform impeccable powers. In light of all this, John says that "no man sinned" (1 John 3: 6, NASB) and that "no one understands God" (5:18, NASB). Given those assertions, they believe sin should be a relic of days gone by. If you accidentally report a transgression, it is a confirmation that you have not been saved because Christians are perfect. In any case, this is not something John points out. We understand that when John says that the proponents are constantly wrong, he is not referring to impeccable impeccability, given what he is creating somewhere else in a similar letter. To the devotees, John says, "If we guarantee that we are not behaving illegally, we are navel and that fact is not in us" (1 John 1: 8). In this way, we are sinners altogether and continue to fight transgressions even when we are saved.

We will never know the complete disappearance of wrongdoing until we are amazed with the Lord, "When Christ appears, we will be like him" (1 John 3: 2).

John, on the other hand, makes no mention of innocence; I do not dispute its meaning that devotees are not constantly mistaken? It simply means that proponents will not renew sin as a way of life. There will be a contrast between the previous way of life without Christ and the new life in Christ. The thief described by his burglary is no longer a hood; he has an alternative lifestyle. The wrong person he portrayed as his inadequacy is no longer a sinner; his standards of conduct have changed. Descendants of God, former sinners, cannot fight nor attack; but he no longer lives as if by example. A descendant of God, a former sinner, may now be struggling with desire, but he has freed himself from a previous indecent way of life. "All who have this presupposition in Christ will be treated in the same way as he is not defiled" (1 John 3: 3).

SO NOW WE HAVE BEEN SET FREE OF SIN THROUGH CHRIST'S SACRIFICE, (WE ARE TO GO AND PRONOUNCE THIS FREEDOM. ALSO, WE ARE TO LET THE PEOPLE KNOW THAT GOD'S FAVOR HAS BEEN PLACED UPON THEIR LIVES AND GOD WILL FIGHT THEIR ENEMIES)

CHAPTER 9

WHAT DOES IT MEAN TO BE FREE FROM SIN?

Isaiah 61:1-2 NLT

1 The Spirit of the Sovereign Lord is upon me, for the Lord has anointed me to bring good news to the poor. He has sent me to comfort the brokenhearted and to proclaim that captives will be released, and prisoners will be freed.

2 He Has Sent Me To Tell Those Who Mourn That The Time Of The Lord's Favor Has Come And With It, The Day Of God's Anger Against Their Enemies.

Prophet Isaiah prophesied in his book that Jesus will come to set the captives free. He proclaimed that captives will be released, and prisoners will be freed. Also, Luke proclaimed the same thing in his book saying

Luke 4:18-19 NLT

18 He Has Sent Me to Proclaim That Captives Will Be Released, That the Blind Will See, That the Oppressed Will Be Set Free,

19 and that the time of the Lord's Favor Has Come.

Sin has unleashed ruin in us, others, and the world. Sin has defaced the picture of God in humanity and presented blame, disgrace, dread. Distress, torment, and demise into the world in the book of Luke chapter 4, reading from verse 18. Jesus spoke this way when He was touched by the Holy spirit "The spirit of the Lord is upon me because he has anointed me to preach the gospel to the poor; he has sent me to heal the brokenhearted, to preach deliverance to the captives, and recovering of sight to the blind, to set at liberty them that are bruised" .Sin brought about our unique precursors being shot out from the garden of Eden. Each human currently has a wrongdoing nature. It isn't just we who are unfavorably influenced by wrongdoing; we harm others by our corruption (Matthew 15:19). To be liberated from wrongdoing intends to turn around these impacts and to ensure that they don't return.

This is actually what God has vowed to do and has just started doing by sending His Son to break the force and punishment of transgression. For those of us who have apologized for transgression and gotten Jesus Christ, independence from wrongdoing has started. We who accept have been liberated from the punishment of transgression, including the dread of death, censuring blame, and hellfire itself (Hebrews 2:14–15; Romans 8:1; John 3:16–18).

We have additionally been liberated from the ruling rule of transgression over our hearts and lead (Romans 6:6, 17–18). Having gotten the Spirit of God, we are given new hearts that want to cherish and obey God (Romans 8:15; 2 Corinthians 5:17). We are not, at this point bound to sin. Paul writes in Romans 6 about being liberated from transgression and a captive to nobility. In Christ, we are allowed to not sin and to rather live honorably. Be that as it may, there is a sense in which we are not yet completely free. We battle with the remainders of wrongdoing found in our old nature or "old self" as Scripture states (Romans 7:21–25; Ephesians 4:20–24; Colossians 3:9).

We don't in any case live equitably, yet at the same time surrender to sin. We are in a cycle of change, bit by bit turning out to be more similar to Christ through purification. In Christ, every one of our wrongdoings has been excused forever. At the point when we sin, our cooperation with God is disturbed, much like an insubordinate kid who defies his dad. In any case, there is rebuilding in Christ (1 John 1:8–9). God never abandons His youngsters and is anxious to reestablish them to full partnership with Himself. Besides our corruption, we likewise live in wrongdoing wiped out the world and endure the negative results of transgression in a broader sense. As Christians, we live between two universes. The current abhorrent age and the guaranteed new sky and new earth. Our opportunity has been pronounced, guaranteed, and halfway experienced however there are more noteworthy things guaranteed but then to observe on the planet to come.

To be liberated from transgression intends to be adjusted to the picture of Christ (Romans 8:29; 1 John 3:2; 1 Corinthians 15:49). Even though this cycle of blessing has started in the devotee, it isn't finished until we bite the dust and go to be with God or until Christ returns (whichever happens first for us). For the adherent to Christ, we will encounter the adoration for God, the tranquility of God, and the delight of God forever, living within the sight of God, our Savior, and Redeemer. This is the reason the missionary Paul could state with certainty, "to live is Christ and to kick the bucket is pick up" (Philippians 1:21). To be liberated from wrongdoing intends to live in an unblemished new world which has not and can't endure the deplorable outcomes of transgression and is populated exclusively by the individuals who have been cleansed and idealized—a world without tears, distress, torment, dread, passing, anguish, disgrace, coerce; a universe of affection; a world vowed to the individuals who have confidence in Jesus Christ and anticipate His return (Revelation 21:1–4).

Up to that point, we live realizing we have been liberated from transgression's territory. All things considered, we are captives to exemplary nature, modestly respecting the extraordinary work of the Holy Spirit in our lives to the magnificence of God. We give God acclaim for the opportunity He has guaranteed and in truth, and live realizing that we have a place with Christ. "For that opportunity, Christ has freed us; stand firm in this way, and do not submit to the burden of slavery" (Galatians 5: 1).

If we guarantee to be without wrongdoing, we mislead ourselves and the fact of the matter isn't in us. On the off chance that we admit our wrongdoings, he is devoted and just and will excuse us our transgressions and cleanse us from all corruption. If we guarantee we have not trespassed, we describe him as a liar and his statement isn't in us. (1 John 1:8-10; NIV). In this way, we need to comprehend what John implies by his remark in 1 John 3:9. The point John is making in 1 John 3:9 is essential that a genuinely born again son of God won't have a mentality of looking to fulfill sin, rather, their lifestyle will be to satisfy the Lord Jesus and to stroll the overall way of the Christian life. Anyway, this doesn't suggest flawlessness. This section states preferably in the NIV over in certain interpretations. In the KJV, for instance, it understands subsequently:

'Whoever God has not surrendered sin; because the seed remained inside him: and he could not sin, because he was conceived by God. Nobody who is a son of God is routinely blameworthy of wrongdoing. A natural germ of life stays in him, and he can't routinely sin- - because he is an offspring of God.' Presently that is a genuine endeavor to be 'free,' notwithstanding; perhaps it is a tad excessively free. The highlight that comprehends here is that John isn't composing something here which he, at the end of the day, repudiates in 1 John 1:8-10. Like Paul in Romans 7, John realizes that none of us are great - a long way from it! - However, in Christ, our life course unquestionably changes. So "can't sin" here is a psychological/philosophical remark, not an actual one.

There is likewise the extra point that a genuinely changed over offspring of God can't be a 'delinquent,' since the individual is presently under effort-lessness, sin done being attributed. This implies that a genuine Christian who unearths accomplishing something 'corrupt,' isn't - and never can be - in a similar class as someone on the planet who dismisses all thoughts of God and 'wrongdoing' - that individual's transgressions are without a doubt recorded and the person will one day be responsible. Some misconstrue these refrains to imply that Christians can achieve pure flawlessness.

All things being considered, John says that "nobody who lives in Him sins" (1 John 3:6, NASB) and that "nobody who is conceived of God sins" (5:18, NASB). In light of those sections, they reason, sin should be a relic of past times. On the off chance that you submit a transgression, that is evidence that you are not saved because Christians are immaculate.

Yet, that isn't the thing John is instructing. We realize that, when John composes that devotees don't keep on erring, he isn't alluding to righteous flawlessness due to what he composes somewhere else in a similar epistle. To devotees John says, "If we guarantee to be without transgression, we hoodwink ourselves and the fact of the matter isn't in us" (1 John 1:8). Thus, we are largely delinquents, and we keep on battling with transgression even after we are saved. We will never know absolute nonattendance of wrong-doing until we are with the Lord in greatness: "When Christ appears, we will assemble unto him" (1 John 3:2). If John isn't alluding to immaculate flawlessness, then I won't conclude his meaning that unbeliever doesn't keep on erring? Simply, he implies that unbeliever won't keep rehearsing sin as a lifestyle. There will be a distinction between the previous lifestyle without

Christ and the new life in Christ. The criminal who was portrayed by his burglary is a hoodlum no more; he has an alternate lifestyle.

The philanderer who was portrayed by his corruption is a miscreant no more; his standards of conduct have changed. The offspring of God who was a previous hoodlum may even now battle with sin, yet he no longer lives as indicated by the example of taking. The offspring of God who was a previous philanderer may at present battle with desire, however, he has broken liberated from the previous lifestyle of shamelessness. "All who have this assumption in [Christ] purify themselves, comparatively as he is unadulterated" (1 John 3:3).

CHAPTER 10

HOW DO WE KNOW CHRIST HAS TAKEN CARE OF OUR SIN?

He Has Destroyed the Works of Satan

Hebrews 9:28 NLT

(Christ is not coming back to deal with sin)

28 so also Christ was offered once for all time as a sacrifice to take away the sins of many people. He will come again, not to deal with our sins, but to bring salvation to all who are eagerly waiting for him.

The context of this verse states that each person experiences one death and the subsequent judgment of God. The main advantage of the new covenant promised by God is that Christ's sacrifice does not have to be repeated, as is done with animal sacrifice. The blood of animals can only temporarily atone for sin and cannot replace man from within. But Christ's sacrifice completely saves from sin as an action "once for all." In the previous verse, this was compared to how people die once, and that this death causes trial.

The Hebrew writer points out that Christ once appeared and died once, and this death was destined for sin. This means that his second coming, which is still in the future, will not cause additional redemption. As every man dies once, Christ will die only for sins. As people die and then be judged, Christ is already dead and will return only to judge the world. The next coming of Christ will be to "save" those who trust in Him. This means that Christ's final return in victory marks the completion of God's plan to judge sin and save His people (Titus 2:13)

Christ was sacrificed for our sins, which made His ministry as a sacrifice for sin final and complete. Christ appeared for the first time to eradicate sins forever, and though He sits at the right hand of the Father today and will one day appear a second the time will come for him to establish his kingdom. His sacrifice for sin was made once and for all - and it was ended forever in Calvary. Just as everyone is destined to die once for their sins — because the wages of sin is the death of every sinner, so Christ once died on the cross and died paying the price for each sin.

He died once to pay for the many sins committed by mankind so that all who believe in His name would not perish but have eternal life. Christ was anointed by God, who forsook sin forever, and only he was fit for it. As the eternal Son of God and as the perfect Son of man, he alone bore the sins of the world and forever removed them. And he returns because our citizenship is in heaven and our Savior is in heaven. Our hope is in heaven, and heaven is our treasure. God is in heaven - and for all who believe that Christ Jesus as Savior, He will appear a second time

His second coming into the world is again a salvation to the world for those of his lambs who are waiting for his early coming. In Matthew 1:21 we can see that "he (Jesus) will save his people from their sin." It was the holy messenger who prophesied Joseph, saying that this child carried by Mary would save mankind. Sin is the thing that isolates humanity from God, and Jesus became the Savior among us, taking care of His crimes, passing the cross. He didn't come to earth to be a charming baby in bed and later became a noble person at Christmas. He came to save us from transgressions, thereby repenting of our wrongdoing. You may ask, "For the cause that I must be saved from error? We find the correct answer in Romans 3:23, where we are told that" everyone has crossed the sign of God's miracle and missed it. "We are all responsible for transgression and asking for a friend who needs help. You may ask," Why should I worry and be protected from transgression? I will simply continue my existence without the absoluteness offered by Jesus. "That the wages of evil sin is death, but the gift of God is the everlasting life in Christ Jesus our Lord."(Romans3:16)

So, if we don't allow Jesus to address the issue of transgressions, we will first commit the crime at the same point, which means the incessant division or condemnation of God. In addition, we will spend an infinite life, which means infinity with God in this wonderful place called paradise. The question of your transgression can be resolved, and Jesus himself, who came to earth more than 2,000 years ago, is Jesus himself, who can save and betray you. Its capacity is so strong that it can be transmitted from the most extreme easement.

Salvation is only prayer. The Bible makes it clear that when we depend on our ability to make the best decision, more sin is simply caught. This is because Jesus is not the main point of our lives at the moment. Similarly, we need Jesus to protect us from the death penalty that results from our transgression; we need His Holy Spirit to save us from the temptations we face every day. We do this by focusing on him and following his driving in our lives. "I said therefore, I have walked in the Spirit, and ye shall not be satisfied" (Galatians 5:16). What an extraordinary guarantee! The more we focus on the Spirit and believe that it coordinates our lives, the less we will fall into examples of transgression.

If all our violations are now forgiven, what is the purpose of adoption at that time? While sin does not affect the ideal cover of Jesus absoluteness on our lives in our lives, it hinders a strong relationship with God and our ability to reflect the nature of his ideals. Sin is reminiscent of an apple wound; if it is not removed, it will spread and damage more and more of the natural product. Acceptance is a cycle that God uses to eliminate the wrong actions of our lives and to clarify the personality of Jesus within us. David was a man in a hurry to confess his unlawful actions before God; he entrusted God to control his transgression and to make the relationship with God ring again. Verse 41 shows how God responds to acceptance: "Lord, show goodness to me, correct me because I have sinned against you. By thy righteousness thou hast sustained me, and always established me by thy attributes" (Psalm 41: 4, 11).

The credibility that David alludes to is a real transgression of him. David was recognized as "a man according to the heart of the Lord" (1 Samuel 13:14). (Psalm 41: 4, 11) The trustworthiness of David is his true confession of his transgression. David was recognized as "a man of the Lord's heart" (1 Samuel 13:14) because he was flawless, but because he rushed to recognize and redeem. "The upbringing of God is a soul that is destroyed; the heart is chaotic, and God is sorry, and will not mock" (Psalm 51:17).

Recognition is how we understand that we have trusted in our abilities, not determined by the driving of the spirit. We redistribute our attention to God and obey the direction of His spirit for our next stages. By the time we recognize Jesus Christ as our Lord and Savior, He will eliminate all our transgressions to the end. All that we have done, he will wash it away by His blood. His repentance complements the fundamental improvement of our souls. We are not oppressed at the moment

CHAPTER 11

WHY IS CHRIST NOT COMING BACK TO DEAL WITH SIN?

2 Corinthians 5:21 NLT

(Christ was the offering for our sins)

21 For God made Christ, who never sinned, to be the offering for our sin, so that we could be made right with God through Christ.

What this verse is saying is that Jesus is the personification of sin, and in His blood, the message of the Cross is written. The death of Christ's sacrifice at Calvary is the greatest proof of God's love for mankind, for God has shown his deep love for us by the fact that, while still a sinner, Christ died for us. The Son of God has been committed to us in sin, and the great creation of the gospel of grace is complete and free reconciliation — unconditional peace with God.

The gospel of reconciliation and all that it means to us is a great and deep mystery that should cause us all, both wonder and praise. "That God the Father made God the Son, who realized not that transgression was done in our name ... that we may turn into the honorableness of God in him. "God, in His grace, extended His hand of peace to the fallen human race through the gift of His only begotten Son, that He might be the Redeemer of our kindness. Jesus took the punishment we deserved to be attributed to His perfect righteousness.

God, in His mercy, bowed to mankind so that the sacrifice for the death of the sinless Lord Jesus would pay the penalty for our sin through faith in Him ... so that the sinful man would be declared righteous, forgiven forever for our sin, and eternally clothed. In the glorious righteousness of Christ. God is clothed with a mortal body in His love, that by giving the undamaged Lamb of God on the altar of sacrifice we may be fully identified with Him by becoming God's righteousness in Him and proclaiming holy in holy eyes. God. God, in His grace, mercy, and love, accepted us as His children and made us Heirs with Christ.

God the Father treated the Lord Jesus as a condemned sinner, pouring out all the power of his anger and wrath upon the Son of his love as he carried upon his innocent shoulders the accumulated sin of the whole world. Jesus was cursed at our expense and paid the price for our sins. He bore the guilt of every man and woman and performed the shocking punishment we rightly deserved so that by believing in Him we might be declared righteous and become God's righteousness in Him.

By acting as the redeemer of our relative, Jesus became the full and ultimate sacrifice for sin. He did not know that sin was committed in sin and was condemned at our expense. He was identified with the fallen race of men and attributed to the sin of all mankind, so Paul wrote, "God has made him a sinner. God did that which knew no sin to be in our name. "Is there no deeper secret than this? Of course, a miracle is of all miracles "God made him a sinner to become God's righteousness in him." Although Christ has identified with a sinful man and has been attributed to the severity of our sin by faith, we are identified with Christ and attributed to his perfect justice.

The eternal and blessed Son of God turned into the unadulterated and amazing Son of Man. After a life of humiliation and sorrow, when He was despised and rejected by the people. He was slaughtered on a cursed tree ... and yet his last words asked, "Father forgive," and all a fallen man must do to receive His forgiveness. The Savior without our sin has become a sin. The Eternal Son of God bore the whole world's accumulated sins, including YOUR and MY sins, upon Him. The Lord Jesus has identified with our sinfulness and shame so that we can be eternally identified with His glorious glory and eternal righteousness by simply believing in the name of the only begotten Son of the Highest God.

Paul makes the central message of the gospel even clearer. This is the same teaching he gave to the Corinthians and many other people around the world. This verse may be the shortest presentation of the gospel in all of Scripture. God has acted for us. It means that God acted out of His love to break the separation between us and Him: our sin. To achieve this, God forced Christ, who had never sinned during his life on earth, to become our sin. Jesus 'death then paid the price for our sin, removing the guilt and removing the barrier between us and God. Instead of "sinning themselves," those who come to God through faith in Christ are honored by the righteous life of Christ.

In short, as a gift of His grace and through faith in Christ (Ephesians 2: 8-9), God accepts Christ's death as payment for our sin and in return gives us merit for Christ's righteousness. Throughout the Bible, from the Book of

Genesis, God taught a lesson. Back in the Garden of Eden, to cover the sin of Adam and Eve, God killed the animal and covered it with His skin. The lesson continued through the symbol of Easter, a prophetic painting of the cross of Christ. God commanded His people to take a lamb without spots or stains, to kill that lamb, and to put blood on the pillar of the door of their house not inside, but outside, openly, publicly, without shame. Think of a man with blood as he applied it up and down on two vertical doorposts and at the top. On both sides, left and right, he drew a sign of the cross. Long ago at the Feast of Passover, God portrayed and prophesied that sin would redeem blood. Blood covers and ensures: "As ye realize that ye were not reclaimed with corruptible things like silver and gold, ye have gotten of us vain discussion, which convention is of your fathers, but in the precious blood of Christ, as a spot without spot and spot:" 1 Peter 1:18.

If you had shed blood under your feet and passed blood, God would not have passed you by. But when you go under the blood, then you will be overwhelmed by the judgment of Almighty God. The sinless Lamb of God is the sacrifice that Abraham spoke of in Mt. Mariah when he said, "God will provide a lamb. Have you ever wondered why such a large portion of the four Gospels is focused on the last week of Jesus life and all that He has done? Because there last week, when the priests inspected the Easter lambs, the leaders of the Pharisees, Sadducees, and citizens inspired Jesus, the Lamb of God. Yet they do not find fault in Him. Even Pilate did not find fault in Him. Religious leaders had to bribe false witnesses to come up with guilt.

When the day of Passover came to the Jewish calendar, two things happened at the same time. Exactly 3:00 p.m. In the temple, the priests tilted the head of the lamb with a small spot and lifted sharp knives into his throat. The Lamb of God, spotless in the cruel at Golgotha at that moment, shed his precious, royal blood for the sin of all mankind. From that cross, when he died, Jesus cried out, "It is finished!" Finally, it is done, all is paid. The priests and the Levites can now take away the knives and go home, their work has been done. Redemption work is done for time and eternity. God dealt with sin through the alternate death of the Lamb of God on the cross. No game of passion can depict the suffering of the Lord Jesus Christ. The tongue cannot say, the throat cannot sing, the hand cannot paint, the tragedy of Calvary and the suffering of the Lord Jesus Christ. Pure and blameless Jesus took the cup with the sin, past, present, and future of the world, and drank it to the end.

The Lord Jesus was in such suffering that small capillaries ruptured. Before going to the cross and the indescribable suffering of the crucifixion, he was already tried, beaten with fists, beaten with sticks, and then beaten, an event that many did not survive. Why did the Romans use the crucifixion? Inspire the horror. The crucifixion had to be so cruel that anyone who saw the crucifixion said, "Whatever caused it, I will not do it. Romans, whatever you tell me, I will do it. But don't crucify me. "That's what the crucifixion was like. Our word "unbearable" comes from the Latin "excruciating," "from the cross. "Jesus Christ drank the cup, the defilement of sin, and wore a wreath, the punishment of sin. The cup and crown speak of the cross.

Jesus followed through on that cost, partition from Almighty God. Not only would God the Father be separated from Him, but at that moment He would become the object of the Father's displeasure. The father must look upon him as a sinner and treat him as a sinner. We now fully understand Peter's text: "For Christ also hath once suffered for sins ..." Friend, that does not mean "once." It means once and for all. When Jesus said, "It is finished," he meant that the debt of sin was paid for all the time. "This man, having always offered one penance for sins, sat on the correct hand of God; from now on, seeking after his adversaries to turn into his foot

NOW THAT WE KNOW CHRIST HAS DESTROYED THE WORKS OF SATAN WHICH IS SIN, NOW WE SHOULD BECOME AMBASSADORS FOR CHRIST, BRINGING PEOPLE BACK TO GOD WITH THE GOOD NEWS THAT CHRIST HAS REMOVED THE CONSEQUENCES OF THEIR SINS FROM THEM, WHICH WAS THE PUNISHMENT OF DEATH AND SEPARATION FROM GOD (So What Does It Mean To Bring People Back To God With The Good News? How Do We Do That)

2 Corinthians 5:16-21 (NLT)

(We stop Evaluating People from Human Points of View. Recognizing we have been brought back to God and have Right Standings with Him through Christ)

16 So we have stopped evaluating others from a human point of view. At one time we thought of Christ merely from a human point of view. How differently we know him now!

17 This means that anyone who belongs to Christ has become a new person. The old life is gone; a new life has begun!

18 And all of this is a gift from God, who brought us back to himself through Christ. And God has given us this task of reconciling people to him.

19 For God was in Christ, reconciling the world to himself, no longer counting people's sins against them. And he gave us this wonderful message of reconciliation.

20 So we are Christ's ambassadors; God is making his appeal through us. We speak for Christ when we plead, "Come back to God!"

21 For God made Christ, who never sinned, to be the offering for our sin, so that we could be made right with God through Christ.

The death of Christ, which paid for the sin of all who believe in Him, led to a radical change. Paul insists that we look at each person differently and often with difficulty. Instead of looking at appearance, an important question to be answered about each person is spiritual. While every human being is valuable and worthy, his or her value is not in physical things or global wealth. Nor can the shallow performance be judged. Their greatest "need" is not for physical things, but reconciliation with their Creator through Christ. Paul understood this understanding when he believed in Christ. He once thought of Christ only from a human perspective. Before conversion, Paul regarded Christ as an ordinary man and His death as a just punishment for heresy. After conversion, Paul recognized Christ as the substitute for the sin of the Son of God and man, as described in the preceding verses.

The realization that every person can be forgiven of sin and transformed through faith in Christ changed Paul's attitude toward every other person on earth. Now he first cares if the other person is in Christ or still in his sin? Do they reconcile with God through faith in Jesus or not? As the following verses show, this is not about Paul, who thinks people are "good" or "bad" because of their faith. Rather, it reflects his deep desire to see people saved through faith. The God of the universe, with all his divine attributes and rights, became man Christ Jesus. The incarnate God was born in the fallen human race. The Creator of the universe came from heaven to earth in the human body. The almighty eternal word willingly became flesh and dwelt among us — and humbly and obediently carried out the Father's word and will in all areas of his life — until his death on the cross. Paul's life was turned upside down and from the inside out because of his encounter with the Lord of glory and because of his immense love and eternal gratitude to God for conversion to Christ and salvation by grace. to follow the Lord in selfless neglect.

It was his love for Christ that forced Paul to ceaselessly share the ministry of reconciliation through the glorious gospel of grace - through which Christ died for all so that by believing in Him we could no longer live for ourselves but to the one who died and rose again. Paul seems to say that before conversion he looked at things, including the Lord Jesus from a human perspective. Records of its actions and performance, however, after his conversion, Paul's perception and perspective of Christ changed dramatically.

And also, his perception and perspective on others. Paul no longer received a human evaluation from the outside. He no longer valued the exterior of the body, which is highly valued by the world today. Because he was saved, Paul valued man more according to his inner character and according to their new position in Christ. Paul knew that if anyone were in Christ, they were made a new creature. Paul learned that the intention of a fallen sinner is unreliable and selfish, and he was determined neither to recognize nor to look upon man outwardly, humanly. He made a decision. Although he knew Christ from such a human point of view, he will no longer do so. Christ was now the resurrected, ascended, glorified Lord of glory, whose personal ministry on earth was replaced by the ministry of reconciliation, where every member of His body is a full and free participant.

Like Paul we must also make sure that from now on the evaluation of others does not take place according to the flesh and our approach to Christ must be not only as a historical personality but also as a crucified, risen, exalted, glorified Lord of glory. Who sitting on the right hand of the Majesty because He is our God and Savior who gave His life for us to live? Living as a Christian can be quite an adventurous. You can hike from treacherous mountain trails, audacious storms, fight the enemy, swim in a calm lake, or take a walk in the pleasant field. There are ups and downs and unexpected turns. While you can go back to the path you took, one thing you don't want on your Christian journey is a spiritual return. Descent means a spiritual and moral return. When a believer withdraws, he somehow enters a less desirable state.

Its validity period can be quite short and unintentional. He can just get rid of neglect, not pray, not read the Bible and focus all his life on God. The believer, on the other hand, may withdraw, consciously choosing to indulge in the sinful pleasures of this life. This type of refusal can have disastrous consequences. It can lead to disgrace to Jesus Christ, who gave His life for us. It can also grieve and bring grief into the lives of loved ones. Of course, backwardness can bring turmoil into the life of the believer himself. He may suffer from guilt or even a feeling of despair or condemnation.

But there is good news for the person caught! God does not condemn him. God's loving care behind it is firm and genuine. The Lord calls that man by the work of the Holy Spirit. We can see this in the comparison of the prodigal son. In the parable, the father saw his son return when he was still far away. But the father did not lock the door and did not demand that the son leave. Instead, the father welcomed his return. But still far away from him, his father saw him and felt sympathy. He ran, hugged, and kissed. (Luke 15:20) The son then confessed to his father. The father's relief and joy at seeing the son was so great that he didn't even blame or blame him. Instead, the father instructed his slaves. Quickly take out the best cloak and put it on it, put a ring on your arm and sandals on your feet; bring a fatted calf, kill it, and let us eat and celebrate; for this my son was dead, and is alive again; he was confused and was found. (pp. 22-24).

The father showed that the return of the son was not a time of condemnation but a time of celebration. And they began to celebrate like the parable of the prodigal son, know that Heavenly Father cares about you and wants you to come back. He does not proclaim the watch of angels to keep your prayers and the crying of your heart. When the Lord hears you cry out to Him, He will answer you in the affirmative. Do not let anyone withhold God, His forgiveness, and grace. Don't let sin deceive you. Over time, sin will bring you pain additionally, don't let uncertainty or blame keep you down, for He guarantees you. The Lord's mercy is new every morning, but don't think you are promised tomorrow. Pray to the Lord now. When you call on the Lord and ask for His forgiveness, trust in His promise to forgive. He will surely cleanse you from your sins and bring you back to communion with Him. May His Spirit touch your heart and give your soul healing.

If you hurt people when you landed, ask for their forgiveness. Do everything you can to eliminate the damage you may have done to other people's lives. Seek to heal and come to terms with broken or injured relationships. Learn from the mistakes you made to back off and decide not to repeat those mistakes. Ask the Lord for wisdom on how to live faithfully as a conqueror. If someone you know is down. It can be frustrating or even heartbreaking when something close is behind. But be encouraged and don't give in to him.

First, intercept the one who cares about you. Link the work of the enemy in that person's life. Be faithful to pray for him every day. Ask the Lord if you want to say something to the person, and if so, what you should say and how you should say it. Always have a loving and humble attitude towards the backward person. Brethren, even if someone commits a crime, you, spiritualists, restore such a spirit of tenderness; everyone looks at themselves so that you will not be tempted either. (Galatians 6: 1).It may be time for hard love, but make sure the Lord leads you and you do not react out of your resentment, frustration, or anger. How to protect yourself from withdrawal. Keep a close eye on your heart. Christian life is about individual relationships with Jesus Christ. Avoid focusing on the list of doses and prohibitions. Be with the Lord all day. Keep your heart and mind in the kingdom of God. First of all, protect your heart as it is the source of life. (Pat. 4:23, NIV). Beware of enemy schemes. Flee from situations that entice you. Reproach Satan when he attacks you. Have a trusted prayer partner with whom you can share your struggles. Finally, let the Holy Spirit guide you, fill you, encourage you, and give you power as you go through the day.

CHAPTER 12

NOW WE ARE TO GO AND DESTROY THE WORKS OF SATAN

By Proclaiming The Favor of God That is Upon Us and That He Alone Has Removed All Our Sins Through

1 John 1:7 NLT

(The Blood of Jesus Wipes Away All sin)

7 But if we are living in the light, as God is in the light, then we have fellowship with each other, and the blood of Jesus, his Son, cleanses us from all sin.

2 Corinthians 5:18-19 AMP

(God Gave us The Ministry of Reconciliation. Telling everyone he is not counting their sins against them IN CHRIST and they have been brought back to FAVOR WITH GOD.)

18 But all these things are from God, who reconciled us to Himself through Christ [making us acceptable to Him] and gave us the ministry of reconciliation [so that by our example we might bring others to Him],

¹⁹ *that is, that God was in Christ reconciling the world to Himself, not counting people's sins against them [but canceling them]. And He has committed to us the message of reconciliation [that is, restoration to favor with God].*

The devil is real and scary. He is much stronger than we are, and his goal is to deceive and destroy. Jesus said, "He was a murderer from the beginning and has nothing to do with the truth because there is no truth in it. By lying, he speaks from his character, for he is a liar and the father of lies" (John 8:44). But Jesus 'death and resurrection overcame him resolutely. The Bible teaches that Christ appropriated human nature "to destroy through death the one who has the power of death, "(Heb. 2:14). Destruction was decisive, though not final. Because of the blood shed by Christ for our sins, the devil cannot destroy those who are in Christ. The reason is that his accusations are no longer valid. The only thing that can condemn eternal destruction is unforgivable sin. However, the cross received complete forgiveness. Therefore, the devil can only kill us, but not condemn us.

The only thing that can condemn eternal destruction is unforgivable sin. However, the cross received complete forgiveness. Yes, it has so much power. Jesus said to the Church of Smyrna, "Fear not what you have suffered. Behold, the devil is about to put some of you into prison to be judged; and suffers for ten days. Be thou faithful unto death, and I will give thee a crown of life"(Rev 2:10). Where is the victory in that? John tells us in Revelation 12:11, "And they overcame [the devil] by the blood of the Lamb, and by the word of their testimony; Trusting in the blood of Jesus, which would cover all their sins, and keeping the faith until death, they conquered the devil.

The devil is conquered wherever his idea of swallowing faith is defeated. That defeat is the cross of Christ and the Word of God. John, who knew the work of the devil so well, said in his first letter, "I write unto you, young men, because ye are strong, the word of God abided in you, and ye have overcome the wickedness" (1). John 2:14). The word of God is a force that overcomes the devil. So it was with Jesus in the wilderness. He quotes Scripture about every temptation of the devil (Matt. 4: 4, 7, 10). If Jesus himself were the word of God and could command demons to obey him (Mark 1:27), and yet he depended on Scripture to point out the temptations of the devil, so should we.

The truth is, Paul says, "In all circumstances take the shield of faith, wherewith ye shall be able to quench all the fiery darts of the wicked" (Ephesians 6:16). So faith is the great conqueror of the devil. "Resist him, believe me steadfastly" (1 Peter 5: 9). But what to believe is the word of God. God's promises, therefore Paul says to Timothy, The servant of the Lord must not strive teaching to teach correcting opponents with gentleness.

Maybe God will give them repentance leading to the knowledge of the truth, and he can escape the snares of the devil by catching him to do his will "(2 Tim 2: 24-26). Teaching is the most common instrument God uses to save "from the snare of the devil." What to teach? "Knowing the truth" is the word of God. The death of Jesus Christ was itself an exaltation and victory brought up by the Son of Man to enter the sinful world, and victory over the forces of Satan, sin, and hell. As we noted in chapter 1, God as the person of Jesus Christ reconciles the world. Theologians are happy to consider how the members of the Trinity have in eternity pledged to fulfill man's salvation. They sometimes call it a "repurchase agreement." But the Bible doesn't quite call it that, and there's really very little talk of an early heavenly agreement about who can do it, who can save them. It is essentially an exercise in useless speculation.

But to believe that God was reconciled in Christ is not speculative and far from useless. Man's sin made him an enemy of God (Rom. 5:10; Col. 1:21; Jas. 4: 4). Man wants to be free from God's love and God's standards. Man's sin, in turn, separates him from God (Isaiah 59: 2). This reveals the strict judgment of God (Rom 1: 18-32; 2: 5-6). From God's point of view, this is not a permanent agreement. God overcomes alienation by reconciling man. This is a great week. God came as (and not just sent) Jesus Christ. God is the mediator of reconciliation. Why? Because sin is personal, reconciliation is personal. Sin is not just an impersonal violation of the "natural law"; it is a violation of God's revealed law (1 Jn 3: 1-10). Sin is against God. That is why reconciliation must take place through God. On the cross, Jesus did not accept the personality-exalting justice of the personality. He met the requirements of God's very personal justice. God suffered a just punishment for (our) sin. Reconciliation is not that Christ pays the debt of our sin to God, waiting to find some reason to judge sinners, but finally appeasing another, his Son, the Father, who did not feel the Son at that time.

CHAPTER 13

ISAIAH PROPHECY ABOUT CHRIST
SETTING HIS CAPTIVES FREE

Isaiah 61:1-2 NLT

(To Set the Captives FREE)

To proclaim that captives will be released, and prisoners will be freed.

1 The Spirit of the Sovereign Lord is upon me, for the Lord has anointed me to bring good news to the poor. He Has Sent Me To Comfort The Broken-hearted And To Proclaim That Captives Will Be Released And Prisoners Will Be Freed.

2 He Has Sent Me To Tell Those Who Mourn That The Time Of The Lord's Favor Has Come, And With It, The Day Of God's Anger Against Their Enemies.

Isaiah prophesied a great sacrifice for the Atonement, prophesying, "Surely he hath borne our grief, and carried our sorrows .Be that as it may, he was injured for our offenses, he was wounded for our evildoings: our tranquility was rebuffed for him, and in his groups, we recuperated. Everything we like about sheep is wrong; we have turned each in our way; and the Lord hath put iniquity upon us all our transgressions. And he will take death to release the bands of death that bind his people. Also, he will acknowledge their sicknesses, that his insides might be loaded up with leniency as per the tissue, that he may realize how to guide his kin as per their infirmities according to the flesh (Alma 7: 11-12)

The heavenly choirs of angels, when he was born, proclaimed, "Glory to God in the highest, and on earth peace, goodwill toward men" (Luke 2:14). Christ's call to all was, "Come unto me, all ye that labor and are heavily laden, and I will give you rest. Take my yoke upon you and know me; I am Roma and low heart and you will find rest for your souls. The Savior confirmed to the Nephrites in the abundant temple, "Behold, I am Jesus Christ, whom the prophets testified that they would come into the world. I am the light and the life of the world; I drank from the severe cup that was offered to me by the Father and celebrated the Father by taking away the cup of Sins of the world, in which I suffered from the beginning in all cases the will of the Father "(3 Nephi 11: 10–11).

These verses are eloquent testimonies of the Savior's divine purpose and service. Today, however, I would like to point out one of the phrases that Jesus read in Nazareth to convey what he is. Isaiah's passage reads, "To proclaim liberty to the captives, and to open the prison to them that are bound," and Luke's quotation reads, "To proclaim liberation to the captives." I would like to share with you this Easter season a few thoughts on how Christ proclaims freedom, proclaims deliverance to the captives and opens prisons to the bound.

CHAPTER 14

LUKE PROPHECY ABOUT CHRIST SETTING HIS CAPTIVES FREE

Luke 4:18-19 NLT

(To Set the Captives FREE)

18 He has sent me to proclaim that CAPTIVES will BE RELEASED, that the BLIND will SEE, that the OPPRESSED will be SET FREE,

19 And That the Time of the Lord's 'S Favor Has Come.

For thirty-three years the God of the universe has departed from eternity into the heavens. He broke into the time zone of the history of the earth as a perfect Man, seeking redemption for all who believe in His name. He was the anointed, who would redeem his people, as prophesied by the prophets of old. He came as an incarnate God a complete God but a full-fledged Man so that his shed blood would pay the full price of the swamp of the sin of mankind. His statements were confirmed verbally and by work after the fulfillment of every prophecy related to his first coming. He was born of a virgin in the small town of Bethlehem. He was the promised seed of Abraham from the house of Judah and the royal tribe of David. The crying voice of John the Baptist in the wilderness would prepare His way, and He would be a prophet like Moses and proclaimed the "Son of God." He spoke in parables and was praised by children. He would be a priest by order of Melchizedek and would be called Nazarene.

He would be a light in Galilee, healing the broken hearts and releasing the captives. He would be falsely accused, betrayed by himself, led like a lamb to the slaughterhouse, but he did not open his mouth to defend himself. He will be crucified with criminals and his arms and legs will be pierced. He will rise from the dead and thus break the power of sin and Satan, death and hell to all who trust in Him. At the beginning of his ministry, he stood in the synagogue of his hometown to proclaim that the Spirit of the Lord was upon me, for He had anointed me to spread the good news to the poor. He sent me to proclaim freedom to the captives and the blind, to release the oppressed. Jesus uttered the fulfillment of this ancient prophecy of Isaiah, and the people there were amazed at the gracious words that fell from His lips, but they tried to kill Him because they could not accept the truth, but He passed through them, His time. Had not yet arrived. Although Jesus was rejected in his hometown of Nazareth and an attempt was made to kill Him, he fulfilled this and many more astonishing ancient prophecies throughout his life.

The Spirit of God was really upon him because he obeyed the guidance of the Spirit all his life, spoke only of what he had heard from the Father, carried out his Father's will, and fulfilled all the prophecies concerning his first coming. He did indeed proclaim the good news of salvation to the poor, believing in him proclaiming freedom from sin, Satan, death, and hell. He gave sight to the blind, hearing to the deaf, and released the tongue of deafness. He raised the dead, turned the water into wine, fed many people, and delivered those who were oppressed through the good news he came to bring. The Spirit of the Lord was indeed JESUS, for He was anointed of God to proclaim good news to the poor; to proclaim freedom to prisoners and the blind; to deliver the oppressed - and he gave his life as the ransom for the sin of the world on the wooden cross two thousand years ago.

There is a little discussion regarding captivity I would like us to consider. I would like to consider four types of captivity. The first is the captivity of physical death that occurs to all as a result of the fall of Adam (Corinthians 15: 21–22). The second is the captivity we experience due to other actions or social circumstances. The third is the captivity of physical disabilities. Finally, there is the captivity we experience in our own choices and attitudes.

CHAPTER 15

TYPES OF CAPTIVITY

The Captivity of Physical Death

All who live on earth will encounter actual passing. Over the centuries, man has tried to dispel the captivity of death through elixirs, powders, cryonics, lotions, nutrients, and surgical procedures. Instead, Christ promises to open the door to those bound by death. As Jacob explained, "Because death has passed through all people, the power of the resurrection is needed to fulfill the merciful plan of the great Creator. Therefore, it must be an eternal redemption - except that it should be an eternal redemption, which this corruption could not have caused non-destruction. Therefore, the first court decision that a man received had to remain infinitely long. And if so, this body must be laid to rot and fall to the mother earth, and no more arise."

For the mortal body to rotten more, fall apart, and cease to rise, is in itself terrible captivity. But without the intercession of Christ, the deliverer of all men and women, the result of our spirit would have been even worse.

Jacob helped us understand this result when he taught, "O the wisdom of God, and His mercy, and His grace! For observe, if the body never again is lifted up, our spirits should be dependent upon that holy messenger who fell before the presence of the interminable God and turned into the devil so that he would no longer rise. Our spirits were to become like him, and we become devils, angels of the devil, to be closed from the sight of our God and to remain with the father of lies, in misery, as he. And how great is the goodness of our God, who prepares the way for us to flee from the hand of this terrible monster" When Christ rose from the grave on the third day as the first resurrected being, he shattered the chains of eternal captivity not only to our body but also to our spirit.

Perhaps it was too easy for all of us to accept this amazing gift as part of a Payment, the one that everyone receives no matter what. And because it was given to everyone, we may not appreciate this gift as much as we should. As we rejoice in this Easter season because of Christ's victory over death and the great promise of resurrection and immortality, let us remember that without this resurrection our bodies would not only be captive to the grave but again united to their spirit, in the clutches of the master of poor darkness.

When Christ took his life again and became "the first child of the most high God" (1 Corinthians 15:20), he freed us all from the bondage of physical death and opened the door to all other miracles of the Atonement. His endless beauty and our dependability and submission overcome demise, and damnation has no capacity to hold our soul hostage. Without interminability, there could be no endless life. How grateful I am for this great gift of salvation!

The Captivity of the Actions of Others

Another form of captivity from which Christ can deliver us is captivity created by others. There is no doubt that Christ has the power to deliver the children of God from bondage. We have examples of children of Israel being delivered from slavery in Egypt; Shadrach, Meshach, and Abednego are saved from the flame of King Nebuchadnezzar's furnace (see Daniel 3: 8–28); Daniel was saved from the pit of lions (see Daniel 6: 10–23)But we also know that there are many, including the most faithful believers, who have not been physically released from captivity. Converted believers, their wives, and children, along with their scriptures, were on fire when early Christian martyrs were imprisoned and eventually crucified or dropped into the lion's den for local entertainment.

How, then, can we understand Christ's promise to preach deliverance and deliver prisoners in such circumstances? Why were all these believers not liberated? It is not always easy for any of us to understand the answer to the question of why because we only gain such an understanding by believing in Jesus Christ (see Philippians 4: 7). That understanding requires, as King Benjamin taught that we succumb to the "temptations of the Holy Ghost and repel the natural man." becomes a child, humble, humble, humble, patient, full of love, determined to obey whatever the Lord sees fit to do, just as a child obeys his father. Those who can obey the will of the Lord, knowing that life is more than mortality and more than we know with limited perspectives, are also able to understand that Christ can liberate the spirit even when the body is in chains.

Every time God's children experience peer pressure to be immoral, to feel ashamed of Christ, or to react incorrectly to any situation, their freedom is tested by the agency of others. The myth that morality and fidelity are old-fashioned and deceptive can imprison more than one person, as generations are affected by choices perpetuated by this lie. The myth that non-compliance with a judgment or charity means that all values are relative and must be given equal weight or loyalty creates a problematic chain that eventually gets stuck in a hesitant and dissatisfied person, leaving him frequently "wind-driven and thrown." (See James 1: 6). But trusting that Christ honors those who honor him (see 1 Samuel 2:30) provides our soul with an anchor (see Ether 12: 4) with which we can respond positively. To "stand in holy places and not move" (Deuteronomy 87: 8) in today's world requires faith, courage, determination, and patience.

The Captivity of Physical Afflictions

Another form of imprisonment inherent in our mortality is illness or disability. Christ's ministry was filled with actions that freed those suffering from pain, disease, and disability. Over and over again, he healed all manner of ailments and diseases. Did the person suffer from "various diseases and tortures" (Matthew 4:24), leprosy (see Matthew 8: 3), paralysis (see Matthew 8: 5–13), obsession with devils (see Matthew 8:16), blood (see Matthew 9: 20–22), blindness (see Matthew 9: 27–19), dead limbs (see Matthew 12: 10–13), or were blind, dumb, lame, or broken (see Matthew 15: 10–13). : 30–31), Christ delivered man from those conditions. From the book of Matthew, I mentioned only a few cures.

Reviewing all four gospels, I have counted more than a hundred references to the healing power of Christ. However, as anyone imprisoned in walls and fences gains complete physical freedom, those imprisoned for bodily weaknesses, whether due to genetics or an accident, or poor care, or a bad decision by us, may not always acquire a healthy body or mind. A man of God named Elder Dallin H. Oaks recently taught that the science of medicine, the prayers of faith, and the blessings of the priesthood could heal the sick. He reiterated that God "is manifested by the power of the Holy Ghost to all who believe in him; yea, unto every nation, kindred, tongue, and people that do mighty miracles. But Elder Oaks also noted, "Faith and the healing power of the priesthood cannot produce results contrary to the will of Him who holds the priesthood. Elder Oaks then illustrates the faith and trust involved in presenting our various pains to the Lord.

He stated, "As offspring of God, knowing Him, knowing His incredible love, and realizing what is best for our everlasting government assistance. . . . I felt it. . . confidence in the words of the chosen girl's father, whose life was taken away by cancer in adolescence. "He stated, "Our family's confidence is in Jesus Christ and does not depend on outcomes. . . We do all we can to heal the person we love, and then we trust in the Lord for the result.

The Captivity of Our Own Wrong Choices

The last type of captivity all people experience is the captivity we create with our agency. Sometimes we sin because of ignorance, sometimes because of our weaknesses, and sometimes because we choose to be consciously disobedient. Regardless of the cause, we may repent and be free from the repercussions of wrong decisions through the love of our Heavenly Father and the sacrifice of His precious Son. True faith in Christ will motivate us to act, to do all we can to take advantage of His grace of redemption offered to us through the Atonement. That faith builds in us such confidence and trust that we want to obey his commandments and live according to his teaching. "By having confidence in Jesus Christ and turning into His loyal supporters, Heavenly Father will pardon our wrongdoings and set us up to re-visitation of Him.

The Savior then organized the righteous, giving them power and authority, "and instructed them to go and bring the light of the gospel to the people in darkness, even to all human spirits; and thus the gospel was preached to the dead. Furthermore, the choose messengers went forward to declare the adequate day of the Lord and to broadcast freedom to the bound prisoners. Despite these sedations, too many of us are reluctant to leave the prisons we have built for ourselves. The Savior knocks on the doors of our chambers, puts the keys under the door, and we often ignore their presence. What forces us to close ourselves in the walls we have built ourselves without wanting to take advantage of Christ's salvation? Are we hesitant or refusing to follow Christ because of the "lightness of the way?"

CHAPTER 16

THIS IS HOW CHRIST DESTROYED THE WORK OF SATAN
By Giving Us Back Our Right Relationship With God.
Which Satan Stole Through

1 John 3: 4-8 AMP

(Christ came to destroy the work of Satan)

4 *Everyone who practices sin also practices lawlessness; and sin is lawlessness [ignoring God's law by action or neglect or by tolerating wrongdoing—being unrestrained by His commands and His will].*

5 *You know that He appeared [in VISIBLE FORM as a MAN] in order to TAKE AWAY SINS; and in Him there is [absolutely] no sin [for He has neither the sin nature nor has He committed sin or acts worthy of blame].*

6 *No one who abides in Him [WHO REMAINS UNITED IN FELLOW-SHIP WITH HIM —deliberately, knowingly, and habitually] PRACTICES SIN. No one who HABITUALLY SINS has seen Him or known Him.*

(Habitually Sins Does Not Know Him).

7 Little children (believers, dear ones), do not let anyone lead you astray. The one who practices righteousness [the one who strives to live a consistently honorable life—in private as well as in public—and to conform to God's precepts] is righteous, just as He is righteous.

8 The one who practices sin [separating himself from God, and offending Him by acts of disobedience, indifference, or rebellion] is of the devil [and takes his inner character and moral values from him, not God]; for the devil has sinned and violated God's law from the beginning. The son of God appeared for this purpose, to destroy the works of the devil.

John emphasizes that those who live inconsistently, ordinary sin have no fellowship with Christ. John clearly states that all sin is from the Devil; it can never be out of a relationship with Christ. All sin in any form is satanic. This verse is often interpreted as a warning to unbelievers whose lives are marked by ordinary, unrepentant sin. The specific context is for Christians. As Paul does to the Romans and Galatians, John seems to refute the claim that the gospel gives Christians a license to sin. Christians should not obey sins. John emphasizes that Jesus appeared to destroy the works of the Devil. This teaching is closely reflected in Hebrews 2:14: "Because children share flesh and blood, he also shared the same things, that he might destroy by death the one who has the power of death, i.e. the devil.

John emphasizes the love of the Father for his children and also reminds us that the love of Christ is a feature of a true Christian. Divine love should be manifested in the lives of all who are born of the Spirit of God. Indeed, He reminds us that the world hates us simply because we are His children, because they rejected His gracious offer of salvation, proclaimed His only Son, and turned the false Word of God into a foolish tale they looked upon.

He also reminds us that we have a living hope in Christ because when we finally see Him, we will be like Him and this glorious hope keeps us pure, even when we are pure, through faith in Christ because of faith in Christ. To Christ, our sins are forgiven and embraced by His righteousness. But it is the opposite of those who reject the Lord Jesus and proclaim His goodness. In the eyes of God, they are not pure but are named as illegitimate, disorderly, and uncontrollable people. They are referred to throughout the Word of God as rebellious, disturbing, rebellious, and annoyed, and John makes it very clear in this verse that anyone who practices sin is also acting unlawfully because sin is lawlessness.

Lawlessness or sin is contrary to godliness and purity, and the unlawful sinner is always contrary to the forgiven child of God. An unsaved man simply does not transgress God's law, but directly opposes Him, so we read that sin is lawlessness. There are two worldviews today. The first view of the world is biblical, and the second is non-biblical. Be God-fearing and righteous - one of God and Satan. There are only two types of people on earth today ... sinners and saviors - those who reject God's offer of salvation and live in direct opposition to His will, and those who have accepted the gift of His salvation. Some are rightly condemned by God and those who are not condemned. Praise God that faith does not condemn those who are in Christ Jesus - whose sins are no longer remembered, who are accepted in the Beloved and embraced in his perfect righteousness.

The inconceivable depth of Satan's perpetual sin lies in opposition to the immeasurable heights of the eternal righteousness of Christ. From the revelation of God to the genesis of mankind, the devil is identified as the mucous source of sin and the subtle instigator of all evil. We are warned that the man or woman who sins is the devil. He is the father of sin. He is the instigator of sin. He is the one who deceived Eve in the beautiful garden. It is a poisonous root from which all sin arises because Satan rebelled against God and sinned from the beginning. Rather than mirroring the integrity of God the Father, he who sins emulates the conduct of Satan. Instead of manifesting the beautiful character of Christ by walking in spirit and truth and remaining in Him and Him in us, they allow the enemy of our soul to dictate what they do and negatively affect their hearts from the Lord. Those who follow Satan's practice and imitate his ways are the "devil." The nature of sin originally attributed to man is inextricably linked to the wicked ways of the devil. He is an instigator of corruption and deception and has been a murderer from the beginning. He is not righteous because he rebelled against the Lord and refused to be a liar and a father of lies.

Although the principle and practice of sin derive from Satan, divine righteousness arises from the Lord Jesus. The perfect righteousness of Christ is attributed to those who are born of God. The new nature we have received from God in the salvation of the Spirit is the nature of Christ Himself, which is attributed to us and cannot sin. But the original nature of sin, which we all inherited from our fallen parents, can do nothing but sin. Our ancient nature of sin is the heritage of all mankind and cannot do good works and righteous deeds. Every member of the human family is born a sinner. Every man from fertilization lives by the very principle of sin, but the Son of God came to earth to destroy the works of the devil.

While man's old nature of sin is the devil, our new nature is God's. The "old creation of Adam" is part of the kingdom of darkness and can do nothing but sin, and the "new creation in Christ" became a child of light and a member of God's family - and this new nature, which originated in Christ, cannot sin.

Throughout life on earth, the believer's old nature of sin longs for our new life in Christ and must be considered the place of death. BUT Christ came into the world to pay the ransom for the sin of the whole world. How we glorify God that Christ was born in His creation to stop the works of Evil. The constant attribute of the devil is evil, and he who sins is the devil. Satan was the one who gave birth to sin and continued sin from the beginning. Human nature is sinful because man is a sinner who was born dead after committing crimes and sins, but Christ came into the world to save sinners and save them from the grip of Evil and by sacrificing his death and glorious resurrection. He destroyed the works of the devil and cut off his wicked ways.

Let us soften our hearts and, in gratitude to the Spirit, let us glorify our great God and Father for His great plan of salvation and wonderful purpose for mankind. His plans and purposes were devised in the House of the Eternal Assembly of the Almighty and were intended to contain the evil intentions of the enemy's attack on the individuals who were made in the image of God. Let us not serve sin and engage in lawlessness in our actions and attitudes, words, and imagination, but rather thank Him for His unspoken mercy and wonderful grace. We will turn away from all that feeds the evil lusts of the fallen by obediently surrendering to God, all that we are, and all that we do. God's purpose for us is included in this precious verse because the Son of God came to resemble a sinful body and experienced the most shocking discomfort, insults, and death, resulting in sin and sickness, want and fatigue, destruction, and death. all that is deceived in the works of unrighteousness and iniquity can be destroyed forever in my life and your life, that Christ may be all.

CHAPTER 17

WHAT ARE THE WORKS OF SATAN?

It Is Sin Separating Us from God

What exactly are the works of the devil? This question is answered by many passages in the Bible, but Jesus gives a simple and succinct response in John 8.44. Faced with hypocritical religious leaders in Israel, Jesus says, "You belong to your father, the devil, and want to fulfill your father's wishes. He was a murderer from the beginning; he did not follow the truth because there is no truth in him. According to Jesus, some of the devil's works are murder and lies. These two sins summarize the nature of the devil and his purposes. He works to see people destroyed and go to hell (that's murder), and he wants to trick them into that destruction (that's a lie). The devil's works are shown in the Garden of Eden, where Satan deceived Eve and led her into disobedience (Genesis 3: 1–6). As a result, Adam also sinned and threw all humankind into bondage to sin (Romans 5:12). Satan lied to Eve with the intent of killing her (that is, separating him from God); he wanted humanity to die.

Before we were saved, we were completely affected by the works of the devil. "He passed on for the wrongdoings and sins with which we stayed as we followed this world's methods, and the soul of the realm's leader left off. The works of the devil in our lives have compelled us to "satisfy the lusts of our bodies and follow their desires and thoughts" (verse 3). It was only through love, mercy, and grace that we were saved from the works of the devil (verses 4–5). The works of the fiend influence humankind ethically, actually, mentally, and profoundly. Morally, the devil tempts people to sin, so evil seems attractive, so people choose evil over obedience to God (James 1:14). Physically, the devil can infect disease, and he seeks to take advantage of physical trials to curse God (Job 2: 4-5; Luke 13:11). Intellectually, the devil lures people into error by teaching false doctrines (1 Timothy 4: 1). He casts doubt and considers unbelievers intellectually blinded by spiritual truth and the gospel (2 Corinthians 4: 3–4). It organizes distractions and promotes confusion that causes people to act hastily, irrationally, and foolishly. Spiritually, he uses every opportunity to rip away the Word of God sown in the human heart (Matthew 13:19).

The devil wants to attack the believers (Luke 22: 31–32). He will try to force believers not to follow Christ to keep them from the ultimate goal of giving glory to God and carrying out His purposes and plans. If Satan can force our love for Christ to cool (Revelation 2: 4) or stop loving one another (John 13: 34-35), then we lose our testimony in the presence of the world and do not satisfy our Heavenly Father. If Satan can seduce us into addictions like entertainment, sex, or pornography, he engages us in the bondage of sin so that we cannot communicate with God.

In summary, the works of the devil must outweigh the work of God. As a murderer, Satan acts against God, who is Life. As a liar, Satan acts against God, who is the Truth. In the lives of unbelievers, the devil tries not to become the saving faith in Christ, so they experience a second death (Revelation 20: 14-15). In the lives of believers, it is the work of the devil to tempt them to sin and thus to silence their effectiveness for Christ in this world. Luckily for us, Jesus Christ came to crush crafted by the demon. As the time of his arrest and crucifixion approached, Jesus said, "Now is the time to judge this world; now shall the prince of this world be cast out" (John 12:31). Jesus did many wonderful things on the cross. He served the punishment for our sins and gave His righteousness. In this way, the devil has no control over the interminable fate of devotees to Christ. Not that the devil cannot tempt a Christian to sin and sometimes succeed, it is because the death of Jesus caused all the wrath of God against that sin, and God does not regard sin against the Christian (Romans 8: 1).

The death of Jesus not only destroyed the works of the devil in connection with our eternal destiny but also provided for our sanctification. Believers have the gift of the Holy Spirit, which inhabits them and leads them to the likeness of Christ. In His goodness, the Lord also gave us spiritual weapons to fight the devil (Ephesians 6: 10–18). The devil can bring us many things, but if we keep fit in God's armor, the fight will be much easier. We need to understand our enemy and recognize when he approaches, "We know not of his plans" (2 Corinthians 2:11).

CHAPTER 18

Christ Came to DESTROY the works of Satan

Hebrews 2:14-17 Amp

(Christ Blood destroyed the work of Satan's power of death over us through Sin. We now have Salvation through Christ and do not have to worry about Hell becoming our home.)

14 Therefore, since [these His] children share in flesh and blood [the physical nature of mankind], He in a similar manner also shared in the same [physical nature, but without sin], so that through [experiencing] death He might make powerless (ineffective, impotent) him who had the power of death— that is, the devil— 15 and [that He] might free all those who through [the haunting] fear of death was held in slavery throughout their lives. 16 For, as we all know, He (Christ) does not take hold of [the fallen] angels [to give them a helping hand], but He does take hold of [the fallen] descendants of Abraham [extending to them His hand of deliverance]. (A) 17 Therefore, it was essential that He had to be made like His brothers (mankind) in every respect so that He might [by experience] become a merciful and faithful

High Priest in things related to God, to make atonement (propitiation) for the people's sins [thereby wiping away the sin, satisfying divine justice, and providing a way of reconciliation between God and mankind].

1 John 3:8 AMP

8 The one who practices sin [separating himself from God, and offending Him by acts of disobedience, indifference, or rebellion] is of the devil [and takes his inner character and moral values from him, not God]; for the devil has sinned and violated God's law from the beginning. The Son of God appeared for this purpose, to destroy the works of the devil.

Christ Came to Destroy the Works of the Devil

Christ came in all the humility and weakness of a baby, but he did not come on a child's mission. John says, "The reason the Son of God appeared was to destroy the works of the Devil". His birth in Bethlehem was an invasion into the Devil's territory to liberate us from our bondage to his works and influence over us. And it's personal; he came to free you from the devil!

He came as our Savior, but he saves us by destroying something. He came into the world to destroy the works of the Devil.

We all are probably for the Devil and his works being destroyed! But just what are the devil's works? Vs 7 says the work of the Devil is sinning, "The Devil has been sinning from the beginning". The Devil has damaged us in many ways, but primarily he wreaks havoc and sorrow in our lives through sin, through pulling us into various kinds of disobedience to God.

The very first time we see the Devil in human history is in the garden of Eden. He seduced Eve and through her, Adam, into eating the fruit from the tree, about which God said, "Do not eat from this one tree". He INCITED them to sin. Sin began as the work of the Devil and according to John, all sin is a work of the Devil. He is behind it, inciting it, stirring it up in hearts, putting the thought of it in people's minds, cleverly scheming to pull men and women into sin. The Devil incited David to number his soldiers that he might glory in the size of his army.

Peter said Satan filled the heart of Ananias and Sapphira to lie to the Holy Spirit.

From the beginning, the Devil rebelled against God and his plans. He incites human beings to respond to God in the same way: to rebel, to say "I will run my own life". The work of the devil is to sin and to keep the whole world in sin.

The Bible does not describe sin as merely a series of mistakes we make, or individual acts of disobedience to God.

Being a sinner is not viewed as merely a human option that any man or woman can freely choose to walk away from.

But the Bible talks about the "power of sin". It talks about being under "the dominion of sin". It talks about sin as a master, about being a slave to sin, and sin reigning over you. AND in this passage in John says, sin is of the devil, and the one who practices sin is of the devil or belongs to the devil.

If sin is a power, that power needs to be broken! If sin is a master, we need to be freed from that master. If sin is a work of the devil, then the works of the devil need to be destroyed! And that is what Christ came to do. It is what he did. He was born into this world to destroy sin or the root cause of our sin.

Not only do we need to be freed from the practice of sinning because it is of the devil, but because it brings such damage into our lives. It is popular to make jokes about the pleasures of sin, "that was sinfully delicious". And there are pleasures in sin. But when the cost of sinning is seen, it is hardly funny. The eternal cost is unspeakably horrible, and the personal cost of pain and misery and heartache, in THIS lifetime is enormous - the woman living in guilt and depression over aborting her baby earlier in life, the marriages destroyed by adultery, the inner shame and guilt from all kinds of sexual sins, the corrosive effects of bitterness, and jealousy, the lives and careers and homes destroyed by alcohol and drugs, and on and on.

The grief and loss and misery sin brought into Adam and Eve's lives and into the life of every person who has ever been born are astounding. Adam and Eve were real people, with real feelings, just like you! Think of them, experiencing the serenity, and joy and beauty and fulfillment of living in God's perfect garden, doing God's perfect will, enjoying incredible beauty and harmony, enjoying daily communion with God, and then, being cast out of the garden, into a world of conflict, death, loneliness, hardship, pain, disappointment.

Adam and Eve's feelings of grief over what they lost must have been profound. Many times, they must have said to each other, "Oh, that we had never listened to the Devil! The cost was, SO GREAT, SO DAMAGING!". And we have all reaped the same consequences. Our lives have been marred, broken, scarred.

But God looked down from heaven, grieved at the destruction the Devil had brought about in the world, in human lives.

He saw us living in the misery of our sin, tempted and pulled into sin by the Devil. And He sent his Son to destroy what the Devil had been doing.

Verse 5 "But you know that he appeared (or was revealed) so that he might take away our sins."

In what sense does Christ take away our sins? Well, we know he forgives them! He bore our sins in his body so that we beat them no more! He became sin for us! That is at the very heart of what Jesus came to do! In him, we have redemption, the forgiveness of sins. We are declared innocent, not guilty, our sin taken from us and placed onto Christ. We rejoice in that! The guilt of sin and the condemnation for our sin has been taken from us! This taking away of our sins is of first and utmost importance! And we should always glory in this and sing about this "taking away of our sins".

But in these verses, he is talking about a "removal" of sin in our daily lives. Verse 4 and 5, "Everyone who keeps living in sin also practices disobedience. sin is disobedience. (But) You know that THE MESSIAH WAS REVEALED TO TAKE AWAY sins". He takes away the penalty of sin, and he also takes away the practice of sin.

As you stand in the safety of the grace of God, in the safety of being declared just, and righteous, the practice of living in sin is taken from you.

You may occasionally sin, but John says this work of Jesus is so powerful that you CANNOT continue sinning. Jesus struck a death blow, to your connection with the devil and actual sinning in daily life.

Jesus saves you not only from the guilt of sin but from the darkness and the misery of continuing to live in sin!

Jesus Christ was born into this world to undo and to destroy this work of the devil, to break this stranglehold of sin and sinning. His very mission is to take away sin!

Many places in the New Testament tell us what these specific sins are that Christ takes away: all kinds of sexual immorality, impurity, drunkenness, slander, gossip, outbursts of anger, bitterness, quarreling, envy, hating, pride, selfish ambition. Titus 2:14 sums it up and says, Christ "gave himself for us to redeem us from all wickedness and to purify for himself a people that are his very own."

This is cause for great joy!! It is the ultimate liberation! We were created to live in righteousness, indwelt by God, and in fellowship with God. We were not made for sin. Sin is like putting sand in your gas tank. It is like putting cancer in your body. It is like breathing carbon monoxide instead of pure fresh air. As John Wesley used to say holiness and happiness go together! To have the works of the Devil destroyed in us is great news!

It is to be on the road to wholeness, to repair, to be. Peter put it this way, "He bore our sins in his body on the tree, that we might die to sin and live to righteousness. By his wounds you have been healed". Dying to sin and living to righteousness is health and healing! Don't discount the physical healing here, but ultimate healing is the death of sin and living in righteousness! Jesus came to destroy sin in your life so that you might be healed!

Jesus did not come just to tell us that we are bad people and that we need to be better people. He did not come primarily to TELL us to stop sinning.

Jesus did not come to condemn us for being sinners. The Law did that. Jesus came to LIBERATE us FROM sin, by going to the root of sin, which was the Devil, working upon us and in us. He came to sever our ties with the kingdom of darkness, AND bring us into union with himself which intrinsically leads to righteousness because he is righteous.

End of verse 5 and 6, "There is not any sin in him. No one who remains in union with him KEEPS ON sinning. The one who keeps on sinning hasn't seen him or known him. John says, if we see him, we cannot keep on sinning!

John Calvin said, "(Christ) puts sin to flight, as the sun drives away darkness by its brightness". Christ is such a person that seeing him and knowing him puts a stop to living in sin.

We know from other passages that we have not fully arrived or reached a state of perfect sinlessness. We still occasionally sin and fall. But the idea here is that we ARE done with sin.

Francis Schaeffer said, "there is not perfect but there is substantial healing". John says the practice of sinning as a way of life has come to an end.

Vs 7 "Little children, don't let anyone deceive you. The person who practices righteousness is righteous, just as the Messiah is righteous. Whoever makes a practice of sinning, is of the devil, for the Devil has been sinning from the beginning".

The logic of this passage is VERY clear.

There is no sin in Christ.

Therefore those who abide in him, associate with Christ, or are of Christ and in union with Christ will NOT keep on sinning. Because we are of Christ! And HIS very MISSION IS TO TAKE AWAY SIN!

On the other hand, the Devil is full-on sin.

He has sinned from the beginning.

So those who are of the devil will continue in some kind of sinning. It may be gross sexual immorality, or it may be more socially acceptable sins like arrogance, despising other people, tearing down others, quarreling, greed, and self-righteousness. Sinning flows out of that basic spiritual connection to the devil that people don't even know they have. So, John says, everyone who continues to practice sin is therefore of the devil.

Sin or righteousness flows out of WHO we are "OF", who we belong to, WHO we live IN! Whoever you are off will determine the way you live! Merely by being in Christ and him being in you, WILL cause sin to be destroyed in your life and righteousness and love to dominate.

It has to. It is the only way it can work. Verse 8 "THE REASON THE SON OF GOD WAS REVEALED WAS TO DESTROY WHAT THE DEVIL HAS BEEN DOING."

This is great news for those who want their sins to be taken away - not just forgiven but taken away! The message is that the Power of Christ is so great that once he indwells you, you cannot go on sinning.

I certainly would not encourage any kind of passive acceptance of what you know to be sinful. But there is a real sense, in which you just TRUST this work to be done by Jesus Christ! It is HIS work to take away your sin! HE came, HE was born into this world, to do that! You RESPOND to him, but it is HIS work. By your union with Christ, sin HAS to go! It has to diminish in your life.

Christ came to destroy the bondage, the darkness, the rebellion, the corruption of our heart! What could we do against the utter corruption of our hearts? What could we do against such a power as the devil had over us? Nothing!

Only Christ could destroy such a hold as the devil and sin had on us! "O holy Child of Bethlehem! Descend to us, we pray; cast our sin and enter in, be born in us today." Salvation is nothing less than that!

Christ comes in and destroys your propensity to sin, your inclination to sin, your love of sinning, your sinful ways of living. Matthew Henry said, "As a justified believer, he is taught and disposed to righteousness by the Holy Spirit. There is that light in his mind, which shows him the evil and malignity of sin. There is that bias upon his heart, which disposes him to loathe and hate sin. There is the spiritual principle that opposes sinful acts".

Why can't you go on sinning? Or to put it another way: How is sin destroyed in me. The answer is the new life placed in you. Vs 9 "No one who has been born of God practices sin, because God's seed abides in him. He cannot go on sinning because he is born of God".

Those who turn to Christ for salvation are "born of God". God's "seed" is the nature of God or the Holy Spirit. The whole plan and purpose of the new birth are to destroy sin!

God's work IN YOU through the new birth, is too powerful to let you stay in bondage to sin, the devil, or the world!

The purpose of this passage is not really to say Christians SHOULD not sin. (Some passages say that 1 John 2:1 for example. I write this to you so that you will not sin) The purpose of this passage is to say Christians CANNOT sin! - or at least cannot practice sin. When Christ comes in darkness must go. Jesus Christ comes to you by the Holy Spirit and inhabits you and gives your life! And he destroys sins and generates righteousness!

Being born of God is work, powerful enough to destroy sin in your life!

If you are born of God there has been a deep, radical transformation within you and there is an INTERNAL PRESSURE created by God within your heart towards holiness and righteousness. You can fall but the bent of your life is towards righteousness and love. You have received a new nature that abhors sin. A new nature to live righteously and in love.

Jack Arnold said, "It is this new nature from God that gives the Christian the desire, leaning, propensity to live a holy life. A Christian cannot sin without a struggle or without a sense of grief so powerful that ultimately, despite his struggles, he will be brought to repentance and a forsaking of sin. Sin is no longer natural to the believer. Though for a time he may slip into it...., nevertheless it is now contrary to his new nature from God".

What difference does this make?

*You are not fighting sin and striving for righteousness on your own! There is a work of Jesus Christ going on inside of you so powerful that you must practice righteousness! Yes, we choose to follow, we make choices to obey, we are not robots, but it is overwhelmingly the grace of God equipping, teaching, empowering.

*You are to have great confidence in the work of the Spirit in you to destroy sin and to produce a righteous living by you. Calvin, "For wherever Christ puts forth his power, he puts the Devil to flight as well as sin".

*You are to view yourself as one who is inclined to righteousness. No, you are not perfectly sinless, yet because you are born of God you practice righteousness. John Calvin said, "Let us know that our hearts are so ruled by God's Spirit that they constantly cleave to righteousness". The power of the Spirit is so effective in you that you must live in righteousness. Sinning as a way of life has been defeated in your life, destroyed. The devil wants you to believe differently. But your relationship with sin is now dramatically altered!

It is wrong to go around in some sort of false humility saying, "I never do anything but sin, fail and mess things up".

That is to discredit the power of God, the work of God in causing you to be born again. It is not biblical thinking.

*You are not in bondage to whatever sin it is that, that you think has you in its grip, anger, sexual sin, some other addictive behavior. Sin and sins do not have power over you, you think they do. Christ did not come to "hinder" the works of the devil, or to "slow them down" a little bit, but to destroy them!!

*You are not under the grip of the devil.

The devil does not have you under his thumb! He is not wrecking your life! He is not keeping you locked up in sinful habits. 1 John 5:18 says, "We know that anyone born of God does not continue to sin; the one who is born of God (Christ) keeps him safe and the evil one cannot harm him." "We know that we are children of God and the whole world is under the control of the evil one." The whole world is under the power of the evil one. WE ARE NOT! The whole world is his – but you are NOT!

*It is clear that Christ not only delivers us from sinning but he puts into us the practice of righteousness and love.

We become people who love it! That becomes the focus and primary mark of our lives!

The joy of the incarnation, our joy over the birth of Christ, is rooted in this redemption and deliverance from sin.

This is WHY we rejoice. "God rest ye merry gentlemen, let nothing you dismay, remember Christ our savior was born on Christmas day, to save us all from Satan's power when we were gone astray. Oh, tidings of comfort and joy...." We rejoice because our partnership in the works of the devil was destroyed by Christ.

For this purpose, the Son of God (came into the world) that he might destroy the works of the devil, in me, in you.

Six things Satan wants for your life

The enemy has a plan for your life: to steal, kill, and destroy.

God calls us to "Be alert and of sober mind," watching out for the schemes of the devil who "prowls around like a roaring lion looking for someone to devour" (1 Peter 5:8). The devil wants to devour our lives, keeping us from the joy of living in a relationship with Jesus.

Six Things the Devil Wants for Your Life

1. For you to doubt God

In John 20, the disciples shouted that they had seen Jesus raised from the grave, but Thomas' doubt kept him from believing in the miracle of salvation. Jesus appeared to Thomas and said, "Stop doubting and believe" (John 20:27).

When the devil tempts you to doubt God, don't let your circumstance determine your God; let your God determine your circumstance.

2. For you to live in fear

Fear is not the absence of faith; it is the misplacement of it. The devil doesn't want to rob us of our faith, he wants our faith to be in anything but God. Life in Christ is life not in fear!

Psalm 34:4 says, "I sought the Lord, and he answered me; he delivered me from all my fears."

3. For you to feel insecure

Don't let the devil tell you that you are unloved or not good enough! You are God's handiwork and, in Christ, we are not only good enough, "we are more than conquerors through him who loved us" (Ephesians 2:10, Romans 8:37).

4. For you to avoid the church

The more uninvolved you become with the body of Christ, the harder it is to persevere in your faith. It isn't easy to follow Jesus in a world that doesn't. When we leave the community we were made for, we are destined to be devoured (1 Corinthians 12).

5. For you to be led astray

"Watch out for false prophets. They come to you in sheep's clothing, but inwardly they are ferocious wolves" (Matthew 7:15). When we rely on the words of men or ourselves in place of God's Word, we can lead others away from Jesus and be led away from His truth ourselves.

6. For you to fail

The devil wants to destroy us. He wants us to settle for what the world has given us and accept our lots. 2 Corinthians 4:8-10 says, "We are hard-pressed on every side, but not crushed; perplexed, but not in despair; persecuted, but not abandoned; struck down, but not destroyed. We always carry around in our body the death of Jesus, so that the life of Jesus may also be revealed in our body." When you feel like you're going to lose, take heart, Jesus already won for you!

Don't want to be devoured? "Stop doubting and BELIEVE!"

(John 20:27).

The Work Of Satan Has Been DESTROYED

www.ingramcontent.com/pod-product-compliance
Lightning Source LLC
Chambersburg PA
CBHW011217120626
46545CB00008B/3025